Art Weithas

Dishonest Criticism

Art Weithas

Dishonest Criticism

ISBN/EAN: 9783744659390

Printed in Europe, USA, Canada, Australia, Japan

Cover: Foto ©Lupo / pixelio.de

More available books at **www.hansebooks.com**

DISHONEST CRITICISM:

BEING A

CHAPTER OF THEOLOGY ON EQUIVOCATION
AND DOING EVIL FOR A GOOD CAUSE.

AN ANSWER TO
Dr. RICHARD F. LITTLEDALE.

By JAMES JONES, S.J.,
Professor of Moral Theology in St. Beuno's College.

JOHN HODGES,
25, Henrietta Street, Covent Garden, London.
1887.

A CHAPTER OF THEOLOGY ON EQUIVOCATION AND DOING EVIL FOR A GOOD END.

An Answer to Dr. Richard F. Littledale.

On the 22nd of last November Dr. Richard F. Littledale sent the following letter to the " Pall Mall Gazette."

THE PRIEST IN THE FAMILY.

There has been a good deal more fuss made over the recent case of proselytism than the incident itself seems to call for, seeing that there was nothing whatever exceptional in the circumstances, nor any departure from the course which would be ordinarily followed by a Roman Catholic clergyman applied to in the manner described. I have known many instances more or less analogous, and virtually the same method was pursued in all of them, inclusive of the factor of secrecy, where that appeared expedient. Sometimes rather more than mere secrecy entered into the process. And it is on this head that I desire to correct the statement made by your correspondent " M. A. B.," who is like most converts in being unfamiliar probably with the system they abandon, and certainly with that they adopt. When " M. A. B." indignantly repudiates the doctrine that " the end justifies the means," and quotes Dr. Faa di Bruno's " Catholic Belief" as declaring that " Catholics do not believe that it is lawful to break a lawful oath or to tell a lie, or to do any other wicked thing whatever, for the sake of promoting the supposed interest of the Church, or for any good, however great, likely to arise from it," and that " the false and hateful principle that the end justifies the means, or that we may do evil that good may come, is utterly condemned by the Catholic Church," " M. A. B." is, I am sure, writing in perfect good faith, but in direct opposition to indisputable facts.

So far is the Roman Catholic Church from laying down any such condemnation as that alleged that it has as nearly as possible affirmed the contrary propositions formally by the elevation of Alfonso de' Liguori to the rank of a saint and doctor of the Church, thereby declaring not merely that there is no doctrinal or moral error of any kind in his teaching, but that it ought to be followed, as it is in point of fact followed, in the confessional, by most, if not all, Roman Catholic

EQUIVOCATION. 5

pastors. And because he is the latest doctor of the Church in date of creation (1871), his rulings are the final ones so far, since no one has yet arisen to gloss, modify, or alter them. What he has to say on the matters at issue is that equivocation, of which he distinguishes three sorts, is always permissible for what are considered adequate reasons. "It is certain," he says, "and the common opinion of all, that it is lawful for a just cause to use equivocation in the manners described, and to confirm it with an oath. . . . And the reason is because we do not then deceive our neighbour, but for a just cause permit him to deceive himself; and, besides, we are not bound, if there be a just cause, to speak so that others may understand. And any honest object for retaining any good things that are useful to our body or spirit may be a just cause." (Theol. Mor., iv., 151.) But suppose there is no just cause, may one then swear with an oath to an equivocation? "Yes," says Liguori, except in a court of law, or in formal contracts. Nor is the exception secure, for he lays down further, when treating of mental reservation, which Pope Innocent XI. vainly tried to make wholly prohibited, that a witness or an accused, if irregularly questioned by a judge in court, may swear that he is ignorant of a crime to which he is in fact privy, meaning thereby that he does not know it so as to be legally bound to depose to it. And if the act be one which the witness does not himself consider a crime (for example, agrarian murder in Ireland), he is not bound to disclose it; nay, more, if only the criminal and he know the facts, he is not merely permitted, but obliged, to swear that the accused did not commit it; while the accused is allowed the like liberty; and those who have thus sworn falsely are entitled to absolution without the confessor being empowered to require the acknowledgment of the truth as a condition. Further, it is lawful to suborn perjured evidence, " if you have a great interest in employing perjury to expose the fraud of another person in order to obtain your own rights." (Theol. Mor., iii., 3, 77.) And as to the doctrine that the end justifies the means, it is the received maxim of the principal Jesuit writers on moral theology. I will cite only one, Busembaum, and I cite him for three reasons :—(1) His book has been edited and solemnly adopted by Liguori, whose acceptance of it gives it all the sanction involved in his own rank as doctor. (2) It has been published at the Propaganda press in Rome, thereby receiving very high Roman sanction. (3) It has passed through more than two hundred editions down to 1876. Now, he says: " When the end is lawful, the means also are lawful." (" Cum licitus est finis etiam media sunt licita," and " Cui licitus est finis, etiam licent media." —Edit. Francofurti, 1653, pp. 320 and 504.) Nor is the doctrine merely speculative. It is put into active and constant practice. Dr. Faa di Bruno's book is a palmary example, being one of the most unverifiable I have ever examined. I will give one instance. In the original edition, he cited as a testimony to a modern Roman tenet a passage as being of the third century, and by St. Cyprian. It is, in fact, by one Arnold de Bonneval, a writer of the twelfth century, whose works are bound up in the same volume as St. Cyprian's in two well-known editions, but so that no mistake can be made. I directed public attention to this trick, and the wording has been altered in later editions, not by omitting the passage entirely, nor by confessing its true date and authorship, but by saying that it is "in the ancient writer found in St. Cyprian's works"—I quote the precise terms from the fifth edition, page 205—so that the point is made that, while there is no longer an assertion of St. Cyprian's authorship, the impression certain to be produced on an unlearned reader is that the passage is in some way connected with St. Cyprian, and of his era.

When I first adduced the citations from Liguori, given above, with some more to the like effect, the " Weekly Register " (a Roman Catholic newspaper) calmly charged me with having invented them, and alleged that not one of them is to be found in his writings. A legal friend of mine was so startled by this that he came to me in alarm to ask if I had not made some unfortunate blunder, by putting one name for another; and I myself fancied for a moment that the numerals of reference to books and sections might have been misprinted, and so have given excuse for alleging that they were fictitious, but I verified them every one. When it is borne in mind that no cause would seem more just, no end more lawful, to a Roman Catholic priest than making a proselyte, the above facts make excusable the conviction that minute scrupulousness about accuracy or about means is not to be looked for when a case of the sort is on hand.

PREFACE.

I AM fully conscious that the explanations on certain disputed points of Catholic theology which I offer to the public in the following pages are in many ways defective and incomplete. My immediate object is to give a reply to a false accuser, and I feel that the sooner such reply is given the better. On the other hand the questions raised are of their own nature comprehensive in their bearings on human actions, and touch on principles that lie deep in the foundations of the moral order. I propose to myself, therefore, in the present undertaking to aim merely at a reply. I hope later to deal with the questions raised on their own merits; to show the perfect harmony that has from the beginning existed between natural reason and Divine revelation, and to make clear that theology has abided by the truth thus doubly verified, and has taught it openly and consistently, and with unswerving rectitude.

I approach the subject under a grave, almost a despairing sense of difficulty, caused by the unreasoning, or rather the carefully-nurtured prejudices of Anglican Protestantism, for the very existence of which the exclusion of Catholic evidence is essential.

The Elizabethan tradition was created to secure this; it has blocked up every access on the Catholic side to the ordinary English mind, it has poisoned the sources of evidence, it has succeeded in stamping its conceptions in the form of household words, and it has strengthened itself by changing the phraseology, literary as well as vulgar, of our language. For example, the words " equivocation " and " dissimulation " have a very different meaning in post-Reformation English from that which they have in theology. In the English sense they are odious, and justly so; but they are put in practice every day by scrupulously truthful Englishmen in the sense in which theology declares them lawful, and yet such is the force of prejudice that those men will stop their ears rather than listen to a theological explanation of their own actions.

Again, it is very difficult for one who has never been trained in the science to know what a theological writer in practical cases is aiming at, whether he is speaking directly as a theologian, or else giving his evidence as to public facts known to him. If, for example, an English moralist were to say that the answer " not at home " was an allowable answer to an unwelcome visitor, he would mean that in English society there was a recognized convention, legalizing the formula, so as to avoid giving a rude or insulting answer. The moralist in question would merely be giving his evidence as to the fact of the convention familiar to him, a convention which, for all I know, has no place in China or Japan, and if so, would be rightly rejected by moralists of those countries.

Where the formula is a true amphibology, and there is a just cause for using it, its use is lawful; otherwise, it is unlawful. In the same way theologians examine whether certain common expressions have in recognized usage a twofold signification. For instance, St. Alphonsus asks whether the words "I say no" have in public usage a positive as well as a negative sense; that is, whether the phrase is simply the equivalent of the word "no," which can only signify a denial or contradiction, or also may mean, this is my plea, thesis or contention; and he bears witness that it is. Viva, a Spaniard, says that it is not. Each speaks to a local custom familiar to himself, and it would be a monstrous absurdity to extend the evidence of either to England, where no such usage is known.

Nor is this all; the questions I attempt to answer in a popular form lie, as I have said, deep in the foundations of the moral law. To bring into Court the principles on which they rest, I must use scientific terms — and rely on their being rightly understood — which in the modern schools of English thought are regarded as the symbols of vagueness or the catchwords of a hazy theory. I have to say much as to principles and conclusions of the law of Nature, for this law theologically is the ultimate appeal and final explanation in every moral problem, as it underlies every true determination of all positive law. Yet what meaning does the term convey to an ordinary Englishman, or what force has its ruling to convince him? Every honest man acts according to the law of Nature and by its light, but a trained moralist alone can explain what it is, what its cogency, what its precepts.

In order, therefore, to make myself understood in what follows, I must stay a moment to explain my terms.

In theology and the later Roman law, that is the law as reformed by the Christian Emperors, natural law is defined to be the dictate of right reason discerning between what is morally good and evil, and prescribing what in general is comprised in the maxim, "Avoid evil and do good." This is the first precept of Nature's law, which admits of no exception, and any moral conclusion not in harmony with it is wrong, and acting upon such is a sin. Here is the starting point of Christian ethics and moral theology, and so far there is not and never has been the slightest divergence among Catholic philosophers or theologians. The Christian jurists take up the matter one step further on, and lay down the fundamental precepts of the law to be, " Live honestly, " "Hurt no one," "Give every one his rights," and from these, moralists and jurists proceed to examine human acts : the former, as they are right or wrong—matters of conscience; the latter, as they are lawful or unlawful—matters of judgment.

The natural law is not first promulgated in the community, and through it communicated to the individual, as is the case in all positive law, human and Divine; but it exists first in the individual, and then acts and reacts in mutual social intercourse. It is a light given to man by, or a reflection of, the Divine intellect shining on the human intellect, and making us to His image and likeness. Theologians explain the fourth Psalm as revealing this. The prophet having announced the first principles of Nature's law, in verse six, bids the people to offer up the sacrifice of justice and hope in the Lord. Then many said, "Who will show us good things?" and the prophet answers, "The light of Thy countenance, O Lord, is signed upon us, Thou hast given gladness in my heart." *

The people of God lived under the natural law, helped with an inchoate revelation, till the time of Moses; then they were formed into a nation, and their new status and polity demanded a system of positive law, but this did not supplant—it supposed, confirmed, and added its own sanctions to the natural law.

The Roman jurists tell us that the positive is sometimes opposed to the natural law, but they use the word natural law in a much wider sense than it obtains in theology. We speak of this law as a body of precepts, in all cases unalterable; they mean by natural law the original disposition of Nature alterable by circumstances. They say Nature has made all men free, but by positive law men may lose their freedom, as in cases of conquest, crime, or contract. Again, by natural law all external goods are common, but a man by various titles may make them his own, and being his own may transfer his rights over them to others. It is evident that in these matters there is no divergence between theologians and jurists except in the signification each faculty attaches to certain expressions.

And this leads me to another difficulty I have to face, and which I wish to dispose of at once. From

---

* I give the words as taken from the Vulgate, because theologians have founded their comments on that version. The more common reading, "Lift up the light of thy countenance. O Lord, upon us," is exegetically the same

the Council of Constance to that of Trent there were loud complaints that the professors of theology in the universities and public academies neglected the practical side of theology, and failed to instruct the parochial and missionary clergy in their pastoral duties. This most important of all the branches of theological training was neglected by those whose office it was to provide for it, and it was thrown upon the Bishops, whose means and appliances were then not equal to the work. In this emergency the professors of canon law admitted, and even claimed, that the teaching of practical theology belonged to their faculty, and about the middle of the sixteenth century they began regular lectures upon it, based on the penitentiary canons of the *corpus juris canonici.* Till late in the seventeenth century practical theology was regarded as a branch of canon law, and it was only in the last century that it was finally admitted to be a distinct faculty, independent of dogmatic theology on the one hand and canon law on the other.

Its tutelage under the canonists has impressed on moral theology certain characteristics affecting, in no small degree, its later history. What is vulgarly known as casuistry—that is the summary settlement of hypothetical cases, by reference to one or two maxims—was introduced by them, after the fashion of jurists when treating of Case law. Theological terms were supplanted to give place to legal terms. Jurists had forgotten to notice the distinction between " fas " and " jus ; " and where theologians speak of "honestum" and " inhonestum," they use the words, " licitum " and " illicitum." These distinctions may appear at first sight trivial, but they are of the greatest importance in explaining the difficulties I have to meet in the following pages.

I will give an instance. There are certain acts which theologians call "indifferent" in the abstract, that is neither good nor bad in themselves, though they are always either good or bad in the individual act, such as to speak, to swear, to imprison another. Morally these acts so considered are not evil, but honest; nevertheless, for their lawfulness in practice, some extrinsic conditions are required. For instance, an idle word is unlawful, so also is an unnecessary oath, or an unjust imprisonment. Here, in each case, the act of itself is honest, but for its lawfulness extrinsic circumstances are required, which in theology are said, *cohonestare actum*, to co-honestate the act, or add to an honest act an honest reason for doing it. The jurists mean the same thing when they speak of *justum* or *licitum*, and summarize the conditions required for the legality of such an act under the term—*justa causa*. Theology says that any good end will free the use of speech from the charge of being "idle," and so co-honestate its use. The jurists could say that a *justa causa* will make such use lawful. I certainly believe, though I am unable to prove it, that the exoatic and clumsy expression which Protestants try to foist upon us, namely, that "the end justifies the means," has been suggested by the theological saying that in certain cases "the end co-honestates the act."

There is a wide difference between the two formulas. The former implies that circumstances may justify the doing of moral evil; the latter expressly stipulates, that the act must not be evil, but of itself honest, although it may need external conditions for its absolute lawfulness. Surely no honest man who looks for the truth will confound one formula with the other. I have studied moral theology for more than thirty years, and I have never found in any writer whom I have consulted either the form of the words "the end justifies the means" or the meaning that they convey. My whole training and study justify me in declaring that this form, in the sense in which it is put forward is damnable and heretical. I believe it to have originated with English jurists, and to have affinity with such expressions as "justifiable homicide." The language of law is generally elliptical, and sometimes amounts to paradox; theological terms are at least verbally correct.

There is another difficulty which I feel strongly, and which needs a bold man to face with hopes of dispelling it. This is the judgment which learned Englishmen have formed as to the nature and history of casuistry, and it seems to be their resolute purpose to know nothing of both but what they can gather from the *Provincial Letters* of Pascal. If this prejudice were confined to the vulgar *literati*, we might hope to correct it, but when the true guides of English thought are subjected to it, what can be done? The influence that casuistry has exercised on human thought belongs no doubt to the philosophy of history, but it is a strange fact that Englishmen who devote their time to the most conscientious study of barbarous or extinct tribes, will undertake to instruct the public as to Catholic moral teaching, without ever having taken the ordinary means of ascertaining the truth of their own statements. Pascal was a wit and a most attractive writer, but he was a violent partisan, and has been shown to be one of the most untrustworthy and untruthful controversialists that ever lived. At least he has been answered, and those who have given a hearing to both sides pronounce that he has been utterly routed. Nevertheless, if we examine any of the usual accounts of casuistry put before the educated English classes, we shall find in them no attempt to examine the nature of the controversy, no reference to the refutation of Pascal, but simply the whole matter settled by the authority of his name.

We owe much to Sir Henry Maine for his studies on the history of law, and indeed in his own field of research he is luminous, and justly regarded as an authority of the very highest class; but the moment he digresses into the field of ethics or theology, a cloud seems to envelop his mind, and his statements may well amaze any theologian. I mention his name because of his exceptional authority, and to point out the difficulty of obtaining any hearing in defence of casuistry, so long as it is disposed of in the way I have indicated.

I will begin by noticing Sir H. Maine's remarks on natural law which is the true basis of moral casuistry as distinguished from legal. I do not contest any of his positive statements. Some theorists may have thought that the law of Nature prevailed in the state of nature or of innocence, or in the golden age alone; or they may have fancied that it was originally given as a written code, or that its conception was exclusively a conception of the Roman jurisconsults. The Antonine jurists were deeply influenced, no doubt, by the Stoic philosophy which regards natural law as the rule of human conduct, but all this cannot account for its place either in Christian ethics or in the code of Justinian. From the very outset of Christianity the law of nature was explained by the Fathers of the Church, following St. Paul, as a law written by God in the hearts of all men to guide them in the way of righteousness, and warn them from evil doing; nor did they proclaim this as a new revelation, but as that which had been naturally given to mankind from the beginning.

The two systems of Pagan philosophy which most approved themselves to Christian thought were the Platonic and Aristotelian. The full recognition of a natural moral law was a prominent feature in both, and it says much for the wisdom and pure-mindedness of these Pagan systems that the Church has found them, on the whole, to be in harmony with the supernatural revelations of which it has been appointed the teacher and custodian.

The conception of the natural law, as the law of right reason, prescribing to men what they should do and what omit, is explained by Aristotle in the first section of his Ethics. He points out that the proper mode of teaching it is the compositive or casuistical as in all practical sciences, and he expands his exposition of it into the examination of the virtues and vices, giving some rules for their discernment. Plato's conception is thought to be more sublime though

less logical. Radically, it is the same as that of Aristotle, but it adds the idea of man becoming by the knowledge of this law like to the Divinity and having communion with Him. Plato's view of the natural law is beautifully set before us by Cicero, De Legibus, Lib. i., v. xiii., and Lib. ii., iv.-vi.

Cicero explains his conception of the natural law, not only as being that of Plato, but also that of the wise men of antiquity in general. This law is divine in its origin, common to all men and nations, unalterable and eternal. It is antecedent to all written laws, and these are derived from it when just, and if unjust, are, so far, not law. It is the law of right and wrong of the just and equitable, to which every duty of man is referred, and by which all are judged. It is found in Pagan writers connected, no doubt, with Pagan systems of religion, but it is independent of them and above them, and has been accepted by the Christian world as the outcome of right reason, and as a proof that God never left the nations without evidence of Himself and of His eternal law.

The early Fathers of the Church wisely accepted this testimony of Pagan philosophy, but they never admitted that they needed it to complete their own conception of the natural law. This they found clearly expressed in the Old Testament before Greek philosophy existed; but as the law was given by Nature, and not by revelation (strictly understood) they explained it by human reasoning, and in the words of the Greek philosophers, and cleared it from such Pagan taints as it had got mixed up with. Nothing was better understood or more clearly delineated in the earliest

Christian philosophy than the law of Nature, and so it has continued without the slightest alteration to the present day, not in stagnation, but in ever vigorous application to the constantly altering circumstances of human actions. From the foundation of the first Universities it has constituted a distinct faculty, and is now taught as a philosophical science, as well as theologically, in the faculty of moral theology, wherever a complete course of ecclesiastical studies can be obtained.

I speak with diffidence of the connection between the conception of natural and the form of positive law. The ideas and proposals of philosophers did not seem to have much practical effect on early law, and Cicero tells us that the jurists of his time did not generally get beyond the Twelve Tables and the Pretorian Edict. After the fall of the Republic, and the establishment of the Empire, the cultivation of Greek learning continued to be the fashion; but the humane and liberal tenets of Plato were no longer suited to the altered Roman mind. The history of the world shows us that usurpation and tyranny, whether political or sectarian, always fosters rigidity of doctrine, and as often as the modesty of Nature has been so outraged, history bears witness to a reaction into the foulest libertinism. The Roman Emperors adopted the Stoic ethics. As they were sages and deities, this system placed them above all laws, and enabled them to address highly moral admonitions and crushing edicts to the mass of their subjects. Naturally the jurisconsults of the Antonine period wove it into their legal interpretations, but, judging from the remarks of Sir Henry Maine, they left, apparently, no clear notion as to the origin or function of natural law.

Yet the Divine origin of natural law, its insistence on the practice of the virtues—at least till perfect wisdom should be attained—and its authority over all mankind, were leading features of the Stoic ethics, and the Fathers found many of its maxims in harmony with Christian morals. In Christian jurisprudence the law of nature has always been conspicuously placed in the front.

Whatever be the exact age of the Apostolical Constitutions, they are certainly the oldest written code of ecclesiastical laws extant, and must have been compiled while the Empire was yet Pagan. We find in them a very clear explanation of the relations of natural law with the law of Moses and the law of Christ. Together with the law of Christ, it is the rule of Christian life, and a sufficient guide without the aid of any Pagan law. Thus understood, it is the $\nu\acute{o}\mu os$ $\pi\iota\sigma\tau\hat{\omega}\nu$, to be studied and expounded to the faithful. Here we have the historical origin of the science of moral theology, and its distinction from moral philosophy. The latter is the study of Nature's law, as known to natural reason; the former considers the same law with the eyes of faith, and as elevated and enriched by Divine revelation.

I have thought it necessary to say this much in order that I may speak to the charges brought against this theology by Sir Henry Maine, who, as I take it, expresses the opinion of the most highly cultivated Anglicans on the matter. He speaks, no doubt, more directly of casuistry, and according to its conception as delineated in the unhealthy writings of the Jansenists; but his sketch of the history of Catholic ethics must be taken as a whole, for each of its ideas is linked with all the rest. He assumes that there was a certain amount of Roman law in moral theology, and that this latter was tinged and influenced by the former. This, in a certain sense, is undeniable, but it needs explanation. During the period (from the middle of the 16th to the middle of the 17th century) that moral theology was in the hands of the canonists, its mode of treatment was much the same as that in use among jurists. Questions were often settled without reference to natural reasons; and maxims, rules, or presumptions of law, common to both codes, were woven together with an approved interpretation of the text, and this was considered enough to solve an ordinary difficulty. Again, as moral theology has for its object to explain all the duties of man, and among these is included obedience to the civil law, and as the Roman law was the law in force in Catholic countries, it became the duty of moralists to explain the determinations of that law so far as they affected the conscience of individuals. But the forms or language of Roman law used by theologians, or its subject matter treated in a moral aspect, never made that law itself a part of theology, or, in other words, I think I may safely say, that theology never was, in the slightest degree, influenced or tinged by it, in its native qualities or spirit. On the contrary, while positive law is always influenced profoundly in its statutes, and still more in its interpretation and administration by the ethical principles predominant at the time, Christian ethics are absolutely inflexible, and have never failed either to bring the civil legislature into harmony with its tenets, or else to denounce its edict as wrong and as no law.

Sir H. Maine believes that since the rise of critical philosophy moral science has almost wholly lost its older meaning ; " and except where it is preserved under a debased form in the casuistry still cultivated by Roman Catholic theologians, it seems to be regarded nearly universally as a branch of ontological inquiry" ("Ancient Law," C. IX.). I perfectly agree with the latter part of this proposition. So far as I can learn, there is no moral science, in the old sense of the word, taught outside the Catholic schools. No doubt the ethics of Aristotle and the dialogues of Plato are read and explained in a fashion in the non-Catholic universities; but to what purpose? Apparently Sir H. Maine is not aware that in our schools of philosophy the ethics of Aristotle are explained in the old way as a science and a discipline, and with the old forms of scholastic disquisition and disputation. Further, this training is intended as a preparation for theology, and in theology the moral science is taken up and explained on the principles of St. Thomas Aquinas and of the old schoolmen. He is not probably aware of the instructions given on these disciplines by recent Roman Pontiffs, and that these instructions are faithfully put in practice wherever the Church has liberty to teach, and the appliances are at hand for providing candidates for the sacred orders with the common curriculum of ecclesiastical learning.

Outside the circle of ecclesiastical studies a great name may be acquired by a new theory, discovery, or innovation as to accepted teaching. Within it fame can only be obtained by fidelity to the old principles, by gathering together and putting in form the wisdom of earlier teachers, or by applying acquired knowledge to new circumstances as they arise. Moral theology has had its epochs of scientific development, and has suffered, like every other human study, its periods of stagnation, it may be, of degeneration. But it tends, like every true science, to perfect itself, and is never retrograde. It may not have to-day names equal to those that once adorned it, but it has their wisdom and learning to support it. It is ever maturing itself, and never before had it a firmer or stronger hold on the educated Catholic mind than at present. Sir H. Maine's opinion as to the decay of moral science within the Church needs reconsideration, and I trust will meet with it at the hands of that distinguished writer.

But he also gives the sanction of his name to a prevalent Protestant opinion which I must directly contradict. Assuming that the casuists are the modern and degenerate successors of the old school of moral theology, he attributes to them the invention of the distinction between mortal and venial sin, and the motive of this invention, he tells us, was not only the natural desire " to escape the awful consequences of determining a particular act to be mortally sinful," but also a desire, equally intelligible, to assist the Roman Catholic Church in its conflict with Protestantism by disburthening it of an inconvenient theory.

I cannot guess to what "inconvenient theory" Sir H. Maine here refers, for I cannot bring myself to believe that he means to give countenance to the well-known fiction of the reformers, that the Church can dispense in venial sins, or can by any means make them lawful. According to this view of our theology, we have a "theory" that the Church or the Pope cannot dispense in sin, but by inventing the distinction between mortal and venial sin we disburthen the Church of that "inconvenient theory." I will not do Sir H. Maine the injustice of believing that he holds that unfounded and insane opinion. I only say it is desirable that he should explain his meaning.

But he is certainly mistaken in supposing that the distinction between mortal and venial sin had anything whatever to do with the Protestant Reformation, except, perhaps, that the Protestants denied it, and in this way it came to be a subject of special controversy, like most other Catholic doctrines equally denied by them. The distinction itself always existed in Catholic theology as clearly and sharply defined as it does to-day. It is a matter of Divine revelation no less than a truth known to us by the law of Nature. It is not my purpose to enter upon any controversy on the subject. If anyone will consult the great pre-Reformation theologians, he can satisfy himself; and if he will consult his own reason he will see the necessity of the distinction. Does not all law admit the difference between a capital and a minor offence? What, for example, should we say of a law that made the stealing of a turnip by a poor hungry man a hanging matter? Yet there are some who represent God as compromised to condemn the poor wretch to hell for all eternity for the act. Is it a wonder that impious men, having such teaching before them, speak of God as a tyrant and renounce His allegiance? It is all very well for well-fed stoics who have no hunger for raw turnips, to preach a severe law to the poor. The poor man, unless he is a Catholic, will think such an act no sin at all. Which system best upholds human morals and law? the theological distinction between mortal and venial sin, or the theory confounding both together. Reason and common sense declare that the distinction is necessary.

Again, Sir H. Maine is mistaken in supposing that the distinction could in any way help the Church in its conflicts with Protestantism. The controversy itself no doubt helped to show that the Reformation was a fundamental apostasy from the $νόμος\ πιστῶν$—the original Christian law. But the meaning of the supposition is that the help received rested on the increased influence of the priesthood with princes, statesmen, and generals, " unheard of in the ages before the Reformation." In these last remarks Sir Henry speaks apparently of the distinctions of casuistry in general, and in this sense I will consider his statement.

I trust this distinguished writer will reconsider the statement as to the fact that the influence of the priesthood was in any sense greater with princes, &c., since the Reformation than before. History proves the exact opposite. What Sovereign since the Reformation has treated the clergy with such deference, provided for their wants with such liberality, or followed their counsels in the reformation of laws more implicitly than the Emperor Constantine? The names of Theodosius, of Pulcheria, of Recared, of Charlemagne, and of several Anglo-Saxon Kings, to say nothing of the Sovereigns who were forced to do public penance for their sins, proclaim the influence and authority of the priesthood in pre-Reformation times. Since then princes have taken their confessors and chaplains, sometimes, also, their privy counsellors from among the clergy. Richelieu and Mazarin ruled France for a time, but in all this we find nothing to exceed what Europe had been accustomed to for centuries. Where we find real political power vested in priests, this certainly was not due to any consideration for their orders or the influence of casuistry, but to personal qualities and statesmanlike training.

In the next place, no one who knows at first hand what casuistry is will believe that it is a fast and loose mechanism for getting rid of inconvenient theories. No theory can bind the conscience or limit the liberty of man. This can be done by law alone, and no amount of theory or opinion can make or unmake a single law of nature. A priest may be somewhat in the position of a jurisconsult whose office it is to explain the law and point out in given circumstances its binding force, and his opinion turns on the point as to whether this or that case falls under it. But the object of casuistry is to guide him in these decisions by anticipating all possible cases, and it must be clear that the more definite and minute its treatment is, the less room is left for arbitrary judgment on the part of the interpreter. Those who mean to play fast and loose with truth, love what is vague and indefinite. The casuists at least have made known to the world the laws by which they are guided, and the rules by which they mean to interpret these laws.

Then, looking at the whole drift and tendency of modern casuistry, it is but little adapted to conciliate the favour or acquiescence of princes and statesmen who stood upon the divine right of kings, and claimed absolute dominion over their subjects. It is well known that from the Renaissance till the French Revolution the theory prevailed in most European Courts that the prince was above the moral law in matters touching his own political designs or those of the State. Catholic theology or casuistry never favoured this. Both insisted on the law of right and wrong being equally applied to all, and their sympathies were as a rule unmistakably expressed in favour of the wrongfully oppressed. Casuists were not in favour in princely courts. They set their face too openly against the counsels and principles of Machiavelli, the day-dreams of King James of England, and the plans for subjugating the Church to royal control, to be left in peace. They were too powerful and unbending to be tolerated, and it is a well ascertained historical fact that the Courts of Europe entered into a conspiracy with the Jansenists and infidel philosophers of the last century, for their extinction. The casuists were constant opponents of Anglicanism, Gallicanism, and Febronianism, the object of all three being to hand over the liberty and spiritual authority of the Church to temporal princes. If the casuists had any influence with princes it was due either to their undoubted influence with the great body of Catholics throughout the Church, or else their uncompromising support of public order and the rights of Sovereigns and all legitimate government, as well as those of private persons. The courtier theologians and their errors are now things of the past: the casuists have seen their teaching approved by the Church without a syllable of it being displaced.

EQUIVOCATION.

Dr. F. Littledale has been again circulating his outrageous misrepresentations of the teaching of St. Alphonsus Liguori and of Catholic theology, this time in a letter which appeared in the "Pall Mall Gazette" for November 18. He has nothing new to tell, and the often repeated story is told in the old way. The theme is, of course, equivocation, and the end justifying the means; the undisguised "end" of the letter is to create distrust of Catholic priests in the mind of the English people, and the means adopted for this end are not only equivocation, but sheer and repeated falsifications.

It would seem as if writers of this stamp felt a confidence that the reply of Catholics would not be listened to by the public, and I fear that to a great extent there are grounds for such confidence. The very nature of the calumnies uttered against us is calculated to deprive us of a hearing, and these calumnies are circulated with marvellous industry. It is well known that hired agents of some societies directed by Anglican clergymen—impostors whose antecedents are best known to the police—are employed to defame Catholic priests, and, in addition to the revelations of their own invention, they dwell unceasingly on the matter taken up by Dr. Littledale.

But there are signs that this shameful industry has been on the decline for some years. Dr. Achilli and Dr. Keatinge have brought their branch of the business well-nigh to an end, and there are reasons to believe that the number of those who will hear both sides and allow even Catholics fair play is much on the increase. The history of the Reformation in England is no longer a sealed book, or rather, I should say, men may now compare the Catholic and the Anglican account of it, and the learned have not been slow or undecided in declaring which side showed the greatest reverence for truth. Again, there is a spirit of inquiry abroad as to the systems of discipline and thought which have influenced for good or evil the morality of the human race, and it is beginning to be understood that no other system has influenced and guided it so profoundly and enduringly as Catholic theology.

I feel some confidence, then, that an attempt to set forth with such brevity and clearness as I can the true conclusions of theology on the matters treated by Dr. Littledale in his own fashion, will meet with unprejudiced attention, and although I cannot expect that Englishmen will generally agree with me, I have some confidence that many may lay down my paper convinced that our theology has been grossly maligned by him, and that it is of itself absolutely blameless.

I wish to explain at the outset that in this paper I do not propose nor mean to follow the opinions of any particular school of theology, but the teaching common to all the schools, from which no one is at liberty to recede, which is adopted in the ecclesiastical courts, and represents to us the mind, or, as we say, the sense of the Church. I must add that I have been engaged the best part of my life in studying and teaching that faculty of theology to which these matters belong, and that I have always regarded St. Alphonsus as my special guide, yet so that I have always tried to trace back his conclusions to their logical principles and historical beginnings, and compare them with the teaching found elsewhere, whether in theology, ethics, or law. I am aware that I have undertaken a difficult task, namely, to explain in popular language some of the most abstruse questions in natural law, and in face of prejudices intentionally fomented against the study itself, the questions discussed, and the persons who explain them. I do not undertake to deal with the matter without having taken the means to understand and master it. I do not mean to imply that I have a thorough knowledge of the learning of the schools, but only that on the matter in hand I can safely give my evidence as to what is and what is not tolerated in theology, and what is the unanimous sense of theologians. The doctrine I try to explain is not my own, as I have said; but the mode of explanation is in some respects mine, for theologians generally write for theologians, or at least expect that their words will be explained by *viva voce* teaching to those learning theology. I have to make a statement intelligible to ordinary inquirers.

1. The morality of an action—that is its rightness or wrongness, its lawfulness or unlawfulness, its merit or demerit—depends on three conditions: the end, the act, and the circumstances. The lawfulness of these three must combine if the action is lawful; a flaw in any one of them makes the action unlawful according to the maxim—*Bonum ex integra causa, malum ex quocunque defectu.* The end is the purpose for which one acts; it is some good to be obtained; and to be morally good it must be in conformity with the end of man, which is the vision of God. It must be approved of God, and in no way opposed to His Divine attributes; that is, to truth, justice, wisdom, &c. It must be according to right reason and partake of human virtues which are participations of the Divine attributes. As a general rule a lawful end is the possession of any virtue, or of any good that virtue stimulates us to acquire.

A lawful act is that which is not forbidden by any law. Some acts are said to be wrong of themselves or intrinsically wrong. Their turpitude is clear to common reason when what they are is explained. They are directly opposed to some virtue, as, for instance, blasphemy, a lie, an injustice. Acts wrong of themselves can never be lawful; no imaginable circumstances can justify them, no power in heaven or on earth can by leave or dispensation make them allowable. To this class belongs all sin, mortal or venial, and to it are added the permanent laws of God, such as obedience to the Church and the inviolability of the bond of Christian marriage. Again, there is another series of actions which are wrong not of their own nature, but only because they are forbidden by human law—*malæ quia prohibitæ*. We are thus reminded of two kinds of human law—one adding its sanction and coercive power to the law of Nature; the other, for purposes of common security or utility, introducing limitations of personal liberty accorded by the natural law. Such, for example, are many commercial, sanatory, and bye laws; and in the Church's legislation, the laws of "mere observance."

The legislative power enacting laws under this latter heading can abrogate or alter them or dispense as to their obligation. In ecclesiastical laws of this kind the law itself allows many exceptions, and does not intend to bind the subject when obedience to the law would entail a serious inconvenience. For instance, no one is bound to observe the law of fast or abstinence if he has reason to think that his health would suffer thereby, nor to attend the Holy Sacrifice on Sunday if his presence is needed elsewhere to attend an invalid. The same principle is admitted in the Common, Civil, and English laws. Casuists moral and legal occupy themselves with the reasons which suffice in each case to exempt one from the obligation of these laws of mere observance, and the reasons judged to be sufficient are designated in each case " the just cause," *justa causa*. So far the general meaning of two technical terms of some importance in this inquiry are brought before us— *integra causa* and *justa causa*. These are expressions borrowed from the Civil law, the first meaning "the whole plea," or the concurrence of all the conditions required to prove an act lawful; the second, " the special plea," or the reason which, apart from general considerations, is held in a particular case sufficient to legalize an act generally prohibited by a law admitting of exceptions.

It has sometimes occurred to me that the teaching as to the amenity and flexibility of positive law in exceptional cases may have given rise or colour to the accusation that we hold the doctrine of the end justifying the means, although the charge is generally so vague that it is impossible to say of what point of our teaching it speaks. But if it refers to the teaching just explained, or rests upon it, the accusation is simply absurd. Supposing an opponent says to me, "Your law forbids you to eat meat on Friday, yet for the sake of your health you will eat it; now to do what is forbidden is evil, therefore you will do evil for health's sake—undoubtedly a good end, and this end you admit justifies the means." To this I answer, If the law itself exempts me, as it does in the case supposed, from compliance with its precept, in what sense is my act evil? or if I am not forbidden by any law to take food suitable to my state of health, what justification is needed for my taking it? A "just cause," I admit, I must have, because my act is against a general law, but this "just cause" is not a justification for violating the law, but a proof that the law does not bind me.

The third condition for the lawfulness of an action is ascertained by examination of the special circumstances in which the act takes place. This is a wide question, and I must confine myself to such aspects of it as I have undertaken to explain. There is a whole range of acts, of their own nature lawful, or, at least, not unlawful, yet from which hurt or damage is foreseen. We are exposed in the course of our lives to many wrongs or other sufferings which it is the right and often the duty of man to guard against, or repel from himself or his neighbour. This can often be effected only by the infliction of hurt, and the infliction of hurt is forbidden by a general law of Nature. I use the word general to distinguish it from an absolute law which never yields to circumstances. It is plain to right reason, and provided for by every law, that in certain cases hurt may be inflicted, notwithstanding the general law as to its avoidance—the punishment of criminals or the amputation of a limb may be taken as a case in point. Such acts as these are " of evil; " that is, to give their general application to the words of our Divine Saviour when speaking of an oath, they are necessary preventives or remedies for evils induced by original sin; are pointed out by right reason as the assigned means for a special end; and cannot, therefore, be adopted without a just cause.

Again, if I do a lawful act for an honest end, and foresee no harm from it, I need no special reason or just cause to explain my conduct; but if I foresee or suspect harm will follow from it, this new element obliges me to special attention, and if I do not avoid the harm I must show just cause for the act. We have then, a clear notion of what a just cause is. It is something extrinsic to the act itself, it does not affect or touch the intrinsic morality of the act; it is simply a good reason for doing an act that without such reason would be unlawful in given circumstances. It is possibly held among lawyers that the just cause is that which justifies an act, as when they speak of justifiable homicide; but this is neither the language nor the view of theology. The act itself prescinding from the circumstances must not be unlawful, for this, as I have said, is the first condition for the integral cause. The justification derived from the circumstances, is, if we must use the expression, the justification of the person who does the act, and not of the act itself. It will be seen from this that the words "the end justifies the means," are the clumsy invention of some one ignorant of theological terms.

There is a special difficulty as to acts by which we co-operate in the sin of another. To explain this matter, theologians distinguish between formal and material co-operation. The former is to induce by any means, namely, persuasion, advice, prayer, or command, another to sin, or to do an act necessarily involving sin. This co-operation is intrinsically wrong, is direct scandal, and can never be excused or allowed. Material co-operation is in doing an act in itself lawful, which, however, another will turn into an occasion of sin. This material co-operation is lawful or unlawful according to circumstances. I am bound by the general law of charity to prevent if I can without much inconvenience the sin of another; but I am by no means bound to forego important rights for such a purpose. St. Athanasius at the Council of Tyre obliged a woman who had falsely accused him to confirm on oath her calumny, in order the more fully to prove his own innocence, and though this was material co-operation, the circumstances justified him in it. To the above classes of actions requiring a just cause must be added oaths and equivocations which are prohibited by a general law, as "of evil," but which, as we shall see later, are in certain circumstances exempt from the general prohibitions.

With regard to all those acts of which I have been speaking, a just cause is always required for their lawfulness; but other conditions are laid down for the integral cause, or absolute lawfulness of the whole action. These acts are comprised under the general designation of "acts from which a twofold effect follows, one good and one bad." The rules for the integral cause are as follows: 1. The end must be lawful. 2. The act (the means) must be lawful or not forbidden (indifferent). 3. The good effect must compensate, that is, must be of sufficient importance to outweigh the bad effect. 4. The means must be suited by the natural law to the end, and in cases of material co-operation the wrongfulness of the act of the other person must proceed exclusively from his own perverse will. (St. Thomas "Summa Theologica," ii., 11

q. lxiv., a. vii., viii.; St. Alphonsus, L. iii., n.n. 59, 63; Gury, " De actibus humanis," c. 11, a. 1, n. 8, 9; Lehmkuhl, vol. i., n.n. 11, 13.) The reader who cares to verify the references I have given may notice that additional conditions are added by some writers, while those I have given are not enumerated by all. The reason of my selection is that I wish to bring forward those conditions only which are adopted by all, though they may not be mentioned in the places referred to.

These conditions include much more than at first sight they seem to imply. They are compendious maxims, the full meaning of which can only be ascertained by those who follow the science to which they belong, and who wish to reach the meaning of those who use them. They are formulas, not intended to conceal, but to stand as the explained expression, in a summary form, of rules constantly applied in the solution of moral cases, where their full explanation would be simply impossible. To make this point clear I will ask attention to the case examined by St. Thomas Aquinas in the place cited above. The question is whether it is lawful to slay an assassin who unjustly seeks to murder us? Theology answers Yes, if only the *moderamen inculpatæ tutelæ* be observed, that is, if the conditions for lawful self-defence be not exceeded.

The Saint explains that by all law we are allowed to repel unjust physical aggression by physical force—*licet vim vi repellere*. But this liberty is restricted by several conditions, drawn from principles regulating the morality of all human actions. The *end* here is self-preservation, the first and truest instinct of human nature. The death of the aggressor is not a lawful *end* of the means taken: this signifies that it must not be deliberately sought for, nor can it be an object of complacency, nor even consented to, except so far as is necessary for self-preservation, or—what comes to the same— for repelling the danger threatened.

Then the *means* must be lawful; the aggressor must have forfeited his right—the right of all men in ordinary human intercourse—to immunity from physical coercion, by the injustice of his aggression; and, further, the means, that is the act of slaying the aggressor, must be approved by right reason as the fitting, suitable, or congruous means for repelling the unjust aggression. I omit other conditions indicated by theologians as required to justify one who slays an aggressor, as they are not to my present purpose. But I ask attention to the last, namely, the fitness of the means to the end.

In the ordinary conduct of life, no truth is more obvious than this, that the means should be suited to the end. A doctor, for instance, is bound to give a medicine suited to expel the disease he is called in to cure; and he looks only at the efficiency of the means. But in moral questions we have to consider not only the efficiency of the means, but also their moral propriety. The slaying, for instance, of a physical aggressor may, under certain circumstances, be allowable, but if the aggression be not physical, but moral, as in the case of a false witness who swears away my life, physical force is not lawful on my part, because it is not the remedy provided for me in this case by the natural law. Such, at least, is the reason commonly assigned by theologians for the limitation in the individual right of repelling injury, as distinguished from the coercive authority of public law; and I give it without venturing to pronounce upon its cogency. We have here a very wide question to examine, easy enough in practical conduct, but difficult indeed to formulate for the purpose of an answer in general and abstract terms. I will try to put the whole case as dealt with in theology with all the clearness I can.

All law, natural and human, has for its object the well-being of the community, of all and of each; so that a law is a means to this end, and so also is every lawful act. But Nature not only regulates our conduct by its laws, but it provides the means suited to obtain its end and ours. These means often fail us, but they are in the world, and are adapted to satisfy every rational want or lawful desire. That these wants or desires are given us by the law of our nature, is as clear a proof of the existence of means fitted to meet them, as the existence of a body is a proof that there is a place where it exists. The fact, therefore, is indisputable, that there are lawful means for every lawful end, provided and adapted by Nature to that end, although not always available to each person. The bounty of Nature may be frustrated by improvidence, injustice, or a hundred accidents, but Nature wishes all to have enough, and each one peaceably to enjoy his rights.

The discernment of this law in the conduct of life is the function of practical wisdom or prudence. To subordinate the immediate end for which we act to the last end for which we were created, and to provide and choose the means fitted for both, this is the great lesson of moral theology and the rule for practice of all the virtues.

This may be illustrated by the case of the punishment of a child, and I select it because it has lately been explained in one of our courts of justice on the same lines as those followed in theology. The punishment of a child is "of evil;" it is not, therefore, lawful to inflict it unless a fault has been committed. Again, it is corrective, and must be suited to this end; and lastly it is an act of authority and can only be exercised by one having parental, or quasi-parental authority. The second condition, the fitness of the punishment, excludes excess, and improper modes of punishment, but it also implies discretion, and points out that affection is called for by the virtue of piety, the bond of unity and love which holds the family together, and dictates to each member of it his place and office in the little commonwealth.

The punishment of a child, therefore, is an act for the lawfulness of which a "just cause" is required, and the just cause is simply the evil to be removed, and the suitableness of the means adopted for its removal. But if we go further into the question, and ask how can one man, even a father, deliberately inflict pain on another, the only answer we have to give is that the quality of childhood, and the training required for it, makes punishment necessary in certain cases, and that the parent has by nature the power to inflict it. Here the necessity is alleged to prove the right; the lawfulness of the end is alleged to prove the lawfulness of the means. In the same way it is lawful to amputate an injured limb to save the whole body, to execute criminals for the safety of society, and to wage war in defence of national rights. Here we have certain practices, in use in every human society, sanctioned by every law, and taught by every moralist, from Solomon down to the last issue of our daily papers.

It only remains to offer the explanation given by theologians for what is shown to be lawful by so many proofs, and is, in fact, evident to common sense. We have, in the first place, to deal with the maxim, "Where the end is lawful there are also lawful means." This points to a principle given above, namely, that when Nature, or, to speak without a metaphor, God plants a desire in the hearts of men, He provides means to satisfy that desire, and that the means so provided are lawful. The maxim does not imply that the means are always available in the concrete, but only in general, and as a provision of Nature; still less does it imply that any means are lawful, for instance, in a case of extreme necessity. The contrary is the express and unanimous teaching of all the schools, and is the teaching of the Church itself; but the maxim means that each lawful end has assigned means for its attainment, and that those means are shown by right reason to be fitted to the end, and as such are lawful if they are honestly available.

The "end" is said also to "determine the means." This merely implies that the right way of acting is first to know the end for which we act, and then to select the lawful and fit means for attaining it. Till we have ascertained the end for which we act we cannot estimate the propriety of the means; for their fitness and proportion is dependent on the end, and measured by it. But we are not at liberty for all this to say that the end justifies the means, for the lawfulness of the end and the lawfulness of the means are two entirely distinct considerations, and we have first to settle whether the means are in themselves lawful or unlawful before we examine their necessity or suitableness to the end. The act done can never be itself unlawful, as I have shown above, but it may be an act lawful or indifferent, which would become unlawful if done in other circumstances. These circumstances comprehend all the conditions for the lawfulness of an act over and above the lawfulness of the end and the lawfulness of the means; expressly the fitness, that is the moral suitableness, of the latter to the former; and they add a third, or it may be a multiple morality to the whole act, having their place with the rest in the estimate of the integral cause. There is another feature in the relations between the means and the end which I cannot omit. I am speaking now of acts of a defensive character only, and I wish to point out that if the expression, "Justification of the act," has any sense at all, it is in the provocation received, and not in the end. We know the maxim, "It is lawful to repel force by force," and it is concluded from this that it is lawful, if absolutely necessary, to repel unjust aggression, even to the slaying of the aggressor in defence of one's own life. But here the right of using force springs from the nature of the injustice done. I cannot resist a minister of the law who legally arrests me, even though I am innocent, and my life is at stake; neither can I use force against a false witness who is swearing away my life. The reason is that force, with its attendants—courage, address, and anger—are given me to resist physical outrage; legal redress is assigned me in the other cases. The means may fail me in any one of them, and then I must submit; but the end, however just and necessary, will not excuse me from transgressing the bounds set me. Self-preservation, "the first instinct of Nature," does not justify the slightest deviation from the rule of right and wrong.

It is generally held that a person who is exposed to danger of death from starvation may take his neighbours' property so far as necessary for the immediate want. I have lately seen this characterized by a learned writer as allowing theft in extreme necessity; but this is not the idea of theologians. They regard property as being in the first instance common, and then made private by various modes of lawful acquisition. But the acquisition is conditioned, and lapses in the supposed necessity to the extent indicated. The starving man, if he observes the due restrictions, does not violate the right of another in taking what is necessary, for the property required reverts to the condition of common property, nor can its possessor be reasonably opposed to the act. I know the English law rules otherwise, and I take it that, considering the state of human society in England, the law is necessary, and therefore to be obeyed. But I will venture to add that the old Catholic custom common throughout Christendom up to the Reformation, by which not only persons in extreme necessity, but ordinary wayfarers were at liberty to take a handful of corn or fruit if within reach of their path, and widows and orphans were allowed to follow the reapers, and pick up the gleanings, showed a truer estimate of the Christian laws of justice and charity than that which the newer standard of morality has made necessary.

I have dwelt so far on one aspect of the general question I have proposed to myself to answer, and I have dealt with it as fully as my mode of treatment admits. I could quote scores of authors whom I have studied, in confirmation of what I say, but I feel I have quoted enough for my purpose, and I am satisfied that I have shown reason and furnished proof sufficient to make the truth clear to any unprejudiced reader. To which I add my own personal evidence—not lightly given or without full study of the question—namely, that there is nothing more abhorrent or contrary to Catholic teaching and the opinions of theologians than that the end justifies the means, or that evil may be done for a good end.

2. I next come to the question of Equivocation, and I must begin by plainly telling the reader, if he is a Protestant, that to understand this matter, as it is in Catholic theology, he must put aside for the occasion the Anglican traditional explanation of the meaning of the word

and of the point at issue, and make up his mind to learn exactly what is the Catholic teaching. This, when all is said, is the point under examination—not whether equivocation can ever be lawful or not, but, whether our accusers relate honestly what we say about it. What is the actual teaching of the schools of theology on this head? The accusation against us is serious, and in answering it I wish to be wholly sincere, and none but the sincere can learn the truth I have to tell.

The whole question regarding equivocation rests on and starts from the treatise on the virtue of truth given by all moral theologians. This treatise first tells us that by the immutable law of Nature a lie is intrinsically wrong, and can never be lawful or allowable, to save the whole world or every living soul. In addition to this, the law of truth obliges all men, by the twofold law of justice and comity, to speak to others with candour and sincerity in ordinary communications, and in answer to a question or casual remark to speak, as the law says, "to the mind of the hearer," that is, as the hearer wishes to be informed. I may add that if the speaker formally or virtually undertakes to tell the whole truth reasonably expected by the hearer, and conceals a part of it, the concealment is a lie, inasmuch as it falsifies the promise.

But if I have made no such promise, and am asked a question the answer to which will be useful or interesting to the interrogator, and I can answer it without any inconvenience to myself, comity obliges me to answer it, and truthfulness obliges me to give the information wanted. But supposing the question to be idle or impertinent, or such that the interrogator has no right to question me on such a point, and I cannot give the information wanted without inconvenience, I am justified in refusing an answer. The case is exceptional in ordinary human intercourse; my refusal to speak causes a disappointment; the law of comity is somehow put out of joint; and therefore "a just cause" is required for my refusal: but I act reasonably, and the disturbance is due to the indiscretion of another. His indiscretion exempts me from the observance of a comity generally obligatory in human intercourse.

But the same case in an altered form sometimes occurs. Suppose that the truth wanted by the interrogator is the private property of another, and the possessor may have a grave reason for keeping it to himself. Further, he has a right to keep it, and no one else has a right to know it, and a refusal to answer will, as I suppose, be equivalent to a revelation of the truth. What in this case is to be done? For instance, a voter has by law a right to secresy in his vote. A tyrannical and vindictive employer wishes to intimidate his men, and coerce them to vote for his party. He asks them singly for whom they intend to vote, and they understand that unless they express acquiescence in his wishes he will sooner or later drive them and their families into ruin and starvation. This question was discussed at great length in the newspapers and in tracts during the two last general elections. It was acknowledged to present a grave difficulty, and a letter in the "Times" implored the luminaries of the Established Church to give some guidance to their bewildered fold for general use. The guidance given, if not very authoritative, was interesting in its way, as enabling us to see the notions of theology current in the Establishment. Two very opposite rules were, however, proposed;

one taught the poor voter to be a hero, to yield up his secret to the unjust tyrant, and to face ruin with a resigned spirit; the other, the more boldly expressed and commonly given advice was, to deceive the deceiver and plumply tell a lie.

Catholic theology can accept neither of these solutions. As to the first, no theologian or body of theologians has a right to impose a heavy burden on the conscience of others, whatever may be their own opinions, unless the obligation is proved beyond all doubt from the fountains of truth. I think this, or I think that, is not the language of theology unless when it is backed by evidence of the sense of the Church. There is not a vestige of proof that a man is bound to reveal (formally or equivalently) a secret which a just law authorizes him to hold, and if he endures moral aggression in order to compel him to surrender his undoubted right, natural reason points out that there must be some legitimate means of escape.

Here we come across one of those perplexities that sometimes molest us in the study of the law of Nature, which, as I have said, is imposed for the moral well-being of our race, and is the expression of right reason. Apart from the prohibition of falsehood, there is another law obliging us to candour and simplicity in our communications with all men, because, amongst other reasons, confidence in such communications, that is, in their sincerity, is necessary for human society. But it is of no less importance that the right of secresy, like that of any other property, should be maintained, and as it is lawful with force to resist a physical aggressor, or with evidence to refute a slanderer, there must be some lawful means of withholding a secret which a man is entitled to withhold, and has a grave reason for withholding.

Where we find an apparent collision between two principles of natural law, both regulating the intercourse between man and man, we are sure to find that one has placed himself in a wrong position and forfeited the right which generally belongs to all. The case of the voter is, in one sense, an extreme case, because as it was proposed it presumed that ruin stared in the face the man questioned; but, theologically, it is a typical case, because, in this matter, theology only deals with the case of a man who has a strict right to withhold information from an unjust interrogator who has no right to the information asked for, and on the hiding of which other rights of the person questioned depend. As theologically proposed, the questioner may be consciously unjust or mistaken as to the nature of the other man's rights, but in any case we suppose him to have placed himself in a false position, and to have made necessary some exceptional mode of action on the part of the person questioned. I have, therefore, to ask the reader to bear in mind that in what follows I have to speak only of our duty to persons who through dishonesty or error have placed themselves in a false position, and have thereby forfeited the right of comity due to all in ordinary human intercourse.

The remedy theology offers to a person questioned as I have supposed is equivocation, but there are two cases in which he cannot have recourse to it—first, if by divulging the secret little or no injury would follow; the mere right, therefore, to hold the secret is not enough. Next, if by avoiding the question or refusing to answer it, he can avert the injury threatened, he is bound to escape being questioned, or to refuse an answer. He cannot then freely place himself in the occasion; it must be forced upon him.

This being supposed, equivocation in its theological sense may be defined as the use of an amphibology* for the purpose of evading an improper question and concealing a truth the divulging of which would inflict a wrong. An amphibology is an expression that has two distinct significations in current and public use, whether as belonging to the language of the people or as legalized convention. St. Alphonsus mentions three modes in which the two significations may be in an amphibology; but they are practically reduced to two, namely, where the two significations are equally current, and where one is more so than the other. In

---

* The term *amphibolia* seems to have been originally used to signify the ambiguous replies of the Pagan oracles, which were so constructed as to be verified in any event. Cicero gives the example—*Aio te, Æacida, Romanos vincere posse.* It was later explained as a figure of rhetoric or a mode of dialectic fence. Theologians, who borrowed the term in its present form from the jurists, have carefully defined its meaning as used by themselves, as a phrase true in a twofold sense, each sense being established by current usage. The lawful use of amphibology, is analogous, not to the "feint" but to the "parry" in sword exercise, for its object is purely defensive, and does not need nor intend that the baffled assailant should go away with a false impression. The object is fully attained if the secret which one has a right to preserve is not divulged; and this generally is the only result.

these—supposing the other conditions verified—and in these alone, is the use of equivocation lawful, so that here we have another limitation added to those already given. Casuists of different countries occupy themselves much in examining whether certain phrases are true amphibologies or not. It is quite clear that these are not theological questions, but matters of mere human evidence. Each author gives evidence as to the usages in his own country, for which his course of lectures is adopted, nor does he dream that his evidence is valid for other places. An English theologian has to consider the usages and laws of his own country, and he would not imagine himself at liberty to apply here what on such matters he will admit to be perfectly true in any Continental country. This is especially true in the case of St. Alphonsus. In the present matter he is speaking of a system of law widely different from that known in England, and he gives evidence as to usages and modes of amphibology known in Naples, but not to us. The theological rule we get from him is that equivocation is never lawful except by use of a true amphibology; however this is to be defined.

This question of equivocation, although it has been considered by the Fathers and early Doctors of the Church, has been imported into theology in its present form from the jurists. From a legal point of view an equivocation is a restriction of which two kinds are mentioned, one in which the secondary signification is warranted by a legal definition; and this in no way differs from an amphibology as explained above. The other, in which the speaker attaches his own meaning to an expression, not warranted by law or custom; this is spoken of by theologians as purely mental restriction, and its use is in all cases condemned as unlawful and a pure lie. So far as I can make out, the lawfulness of this kind of restriction was first formally asserted by the jurist Navarre; it is said to have been introduced to the notice of theologians by Sanchez, who, however, declares it suspected. It seems to have been approved by a few of the Summists in the seventeenth century, was condemned by Innocent XI., and since then has been rejected by all Catholic writers.

St. Alphonsus, like many other theologians, reproduces the old language of Navarre, although corrected in several respects on the lines marked out by the condemnations of Innocent. His mode of treatment, therefore, is rather legal than theological; he does not speak of equivocation so much for its own sake as to explain the crime of perjury: he indicates rather than explains the several conditions required for its lawful use, and his phraseology must be understood rather in its legal than its theological sense. He says, for instance, that the just cause of equivocation may be any honest end for retaining our goods. Here he adopts the formula of Navarre and corrects it, for the latter included in the just cause of equivocation whatever is necessary or useful for the doing of any virtuous act. This St. Alphonsus rejects, clearly on account of the second condemnation of Innocent, but in reproducing the formula he strays verbally from the strict legal terms. Navarre says: " A just cause of using these amphibologies is *whenever* it is necessary or useful," &c. St. Alphonsus puts it: " The just cause may be the honest end," &c.

I have said that the just cause is not the end, although it includes it. Navarre therefore is, in the words last quoted, technically more accurate than St. Alphonsus, but no theologian can mistake the meaning of the latter. He confines himself to the case of one who has a right to hide a secret, who endures unjust aggression in an attempt made to extort it, and who nevertheless cannot lawfully use equivocation unless the defence of his further rights require this. The last and crowning condition he speaks of by an ellipsis as the "just cause." In reality his words express a new limitation on the lawfulness of equivocation, confining it to the defence of lawful rights unjustly threatened.

If the reader wishes to pursue this subject further, he will find what I have laid down, and much more, unmistakably indicated in the theology of St. Alphonsus (L. iv., n.n. 151-174), or should any obscurity remain, the numerous writers cited by him will be found more explicit. I have only to add for myself that the doctrine of equivocation, with the numerous limitations imposed upon its use as given above, is the common teaching of Catholic theology, and that I do not know a single author who in any particular dissents from it as so explained. Before leaving this matter, I will briefly enumerate the limitations insisted on by theologians in the use of equivocation. 1. The use is never lawful in order to obtrude or suggest an untruth. 2. The deception of the hearers can never be intended, nor the speech such as will of itself cause it. 3. The amphibology must be truly such, having two acknowledged significations, presumedly known to the hearers; a purely mental restriction can never be used. 4. An amphibology can only be used to hide a secret which the speaker has a strict right to hide, and which the interrogator has no right to know; 5, when on its concealment other rights of some importance depend; 6, and when the occasion is not freely chosen, but forced on one; 7, or when a refusal to answer will suffice.

The reasons given by theologians for the lawfulness of equivocation under these several restrictions are: 1. The hearer has put himself in a false position, and forfeited his claim to comity. 2. The preservation of secrets is an important right necessary for human society; it belongs to the virtue of prudence to guard them, and the laws of human intercourse must provide lawful means for doing so, while there is no other that can be proposed. 3. An amphibology is a true statement where there is no wish to deceive. 4. No wrong is done by simply withholding what another has no right to.

This, then, being the teaching of St. Alphonsus and of Catholic theology, it is time to examine Dr. Littledale's exposition of it. This gentleman writes as follows in his letter to the "Pall Mall Gazette": "What he (Liguori) has to say on these matters (that the end justifies the means) is that equivocation, of which he distinguishes three sorts, is always permissible for what are considered adequate reasons. 'It is certain,' he says, 'and the common opinion of all that it is lawful for a just cause to use equivocation in the manner described, and to confirm it with an oath, . . . and the reason is because we do not then deceive our neighbour, but for a just cause permit him to deceive himself, and besides we are not bound, if there be a just cause, to speak so that others may understand. And any honest object for retaining any good things that are useful to our body or soul may be a just cause.'"

St. Alphonsus has said nothing "on the

matter at issue," for he probably never heard of the absurd formula of the end justifying the means or the inferences drawn from it; but his whole teaching is abhorrent from its conception, and expressly condemns it. I have already spoken of his teaching and the common doctrine on the relations between the end and means; a few words will, therefore, suffice here to bring out his meaning more expressly. He requires a threefold rectitude in every act that it should be good, *ex integra causa*, the absence of any one of which renders the act unlawful. They are the goodness of the object (the act itself or the means), the goodness of the end, and, lastly, the goodness of the circumstances. Of these, the goodness or badness of the object or means is the *essential* goodness or badness of the act, and that which has first to be considered; the other considerations are accessory. It ought to be clear to anyone who ventures on interpreting theological language that what is *essential* to anything can never under any circumstances be separated from it or change its nature. If, therefore, certain " means " be of themselves unlawful, their adoption is essentially wrong, and can in no hypothesis be lawful. In treating of

F

equivocation, theologians begin by explaining (unless when they take it for granted) that the act is in itself not unlawful. This admitted, they have only from the end and circumstance to point out the integral cause. In the same way they declare that a lie can in no possible hypothesis be lawful, because a lie is intrinsically wrong (*Cf.* St. Alphonsus, L. ii., n.n. 36-39).

In the next place, St. Alphonsus does not distinguish or describe three "sorts" or "manners" of equivocation. His distinction regards the "modes" of amphibology—a very different thing. If he does make a distinction between different kinds of equivocations, it is between those that are lawful and unlawful, or, what comes to the same, between those in which a true amphibology is used and purely mental restrictions, which he declares unlawful. Thirdly, he never says nor implies that "equivocation, &c., &c., is always permissible, &c." The limitations I have drawn from his words show that it is lawful only in exceedingly difficult and exceptional cases. Fourthly, Dr. Littledale's expression, "for what are considered adequate reasons," is an excellent instance of an unlawful equivocation. A "just cause" may be spoken of, though not accurately, as "adequate reasons," but St. Alphonsus gives it a distinct theological sense and amplitude; his accuser later gives his readers to understand that each one is at liberty to settle for himself what is a just cause; and hence we have the convenient words, "*what may be thought* adequate reasons," that is in the sense later put upon them—which any crafty impostor or desperate criminal may think adequate reasons. I pass over the absurd expression, "the common opinion of all," which St. Alphonsus does not use, as it is not to the purpose, and only shows the inexact and unscholarlike hand of the translator.

Fifthly, coming to the translation itself, we have twice the words "*ex justa causa*" rendered "for a just cause," and "*si causa justa subsit*" given "if there be a just cause." These three mistranslations may seem a trifle, but they are very useful to the translator who is bent on making a "just cause" the equivalent of a "good end." In the two first examples they should be "from a just cause," and in the last "if a just cause underlies." I have said that

St. Alphonsus by an ellipsis speaks of a special just cause as a special honest end, but the words here in question show his meaning. No one speaks of an action done *from* a good end, but only from provocation and necessity.

Sixthly, the words of St. Alphonsus, "*et ex alia parte non tenemur ad mentem aliorum loqui,*" should be rendered, "And on the other side (that of the unjust interrogators) we are not bound to speak to their mind," that is, to give them the knowledge they try to extort from us. I have spoken already of this special limitation, and of the meaning of the words "to speak to the mind of others." A man may forfeit this right, and give just cause for its being denied him, but if it is refused by a lawful equivocation the hearer "may understand;" and what is plainly suggested by Dr. Littledale's words, that in general we are not bound to speak so that others "may understand," is without any foundation even in the exceptional case of an unjust interrogator. Here in a few lines taken from this writer we have about half a score of flat misrepresentations of the teaching of St. Alphonsus, and it strikes me that this performance is hardly above his average. He proceeds:

"But suppose there is no just cause, may one then swear with an oath (sic) to an equivocation? 'Yes,' says Liguori, 'except in a Court of law or in formal contracts.'" So says Dr. Littledale; but in fact St. Alphonsus never proposes any such question, nor gives any such answer; his express teaching, and that of every theologian, answers No to the question invented by Dr. Littledale. In the first place, the Saint does not question whether such an oath is lawful or not, but whether it is a mortal or a venial sin. This implies that it is in all cases a sin and may never be taken. Perhaps Dr. Littledale thinks with other Anglicans that a venial sin "may" be committed for a good end, or some necessity, or that the Pope can give a dispensation to commit it. We cannot permit these monstrous opinions to be imputed to us, but I can assure the non-Catholic reader that in our theology a venial sin is a greater evil than any possible human calamity short of sin; that no necessity whatever can make it lawful; that no power in heaven or on earth can give leave to commit it; and that no good end can justify it. But whatever be the opinions of non-Catholics on this subject, St. Alphonsus does not say what he is represented to say. He says that such an oath is always sinful, and, therefore, may never be taken. As to the question of the gravity of the sin, which alone he considers, he does not even give a decided judgment. He gives the two opposite opinions, and thinks the milder opinion more probable. The " yes " of Dr. Littledale's exposition, with its quotation marks, makes it doubly deceptive.

Again, St. Alphonsus is not speaking of the just cause of an equivocation, which matter he had settled in the previous paragraph, but of the just cause of an oath—quite a different matter—which he had explained in the previous chapter, n.n. 144-150. Thus we find three misrepresentations at least in these two lines of Dr. Littledale's letter. But I must leave for a little this curious letter that I may explain our theology on the new subject it introduces—the nature and obligations of an oath.

3. The fathers and theologians, examining the conditions for a lawful oath, follow the precept given in Jeremias iv., 2, " You shall swear, the Lord liveth, in truth, in judgment, and in justice." The first condition, then, for a lawful oath is truth; its violation is always a grievous

crime, and constitutes perjury. The second condition is judgment; this means due reverence in the act, and a necessity for it, that is, a just cause or ground for invoking the witness of God to our statement. If the irreverence is slight or not wholly wilful, or if the necessity is rashly presumed, the sin so far is not grievous, but venial. If, on the other hand, the irreverence is great, as, for instance, profanity in the form of swearing in confirmation of any truth however trifling, the sin is mortal, and though not strictly a perjury, is nevertheless a sacrilege. In this sense theologians say that the mere defect of "judgment" by itself does not exceed a venial sin. The third condition, "justice," provides that no wrong shall be spoken, and that no promise to do wrong shall be contained in the oath. Saving the other conditions, the degree of sin in defect of justice is measured by the injury foreseen, and a promise under oath to do that which is wrong in any respect is not binding, nor is that which is so promised covered by the oath.

Returning to the proposition of St. Alphonsus so grossly misrepresented by Dr. Littledale, we find the question, " Is it a mortal sin to swear to an amphibology or restriction not purely mental, as below, without a just cause?" And, "below," he gives the reason for the more probable negative opinion: "The reason of this more probable opinion is because in this kind of oath truth and justice are present; it fails only in judgment or discretion, which defect is only venial." In the hypothesis, the only defect of the oath is that it is taken without necessity, and he excepts oaths taken in contracts and courts of law, because then judgment and discretion are more strictly required. Dr. Littledale proceeds —

"Nor is the exception secure, for he lays down further, when treating of mental reservation, which Pope Innocent XI. vainly tried to make wholly prohibited, that a witness or an accused, if irregularly questioned by a judge in a court, may swear that he is ignorant of a crime to which he is in fact privy, meaning thereby that he does not know it so as to be legally bound to depose to it. And if the act be one which the witness does not himself consider a crime (for example, agrarian murder in Ireland), he is not bound to declare it; nay, more, if only the criminal and he know the facts, he is not merely permitted, but obliged to swear that the accused did not commit it; while the accused is allowed the like liberty; and those who have thus sworn falsely are entitled to absolution without the confessor being empowered to require the acknowledgment of the truth as a condition."

All this sounds very horrible and alarming if we bear in mind the allusion to agrarian crime in Ireland, and the suggestion now frequently repeated in certain quarters, that the Catholic clergy of Ireland use their sacred office to screen or encourage crime. What is more, anyone unacquainted with theology or law, though he might not jumble up matters as Dr. Littledale does, would most likely feel greatly perplexed reading what St. Alphonsus says on these matters. The question appears to me too serious to occupy the reader mainly with Dr. Littledale's misrepresentations, and I propose, therefore, to set forth, in answer to them, the true teaching of Catholic theology.

From the formation of Christendom until the beginning of this century, and consequently at the date when St. Alphonsus wrote, it may be said that, at least as regards judicial procedure, there were but two laws known throughout Catholic Europe — the canon law and the Roman or civil law. These were the two common laws; they were publicly taught in all the universities and practised in all courts. Each country had its own special laws, modifying to a great extent the common laws; but, as I have said, the judicial procedure, so far at least as regards the examining of the accused and witnesses, was in many respects the same in all Europe. In England, in the reign of Elizabeth and James the First, we find the Roman law, so far as it favours witnesses and accused, openly quoted in the High Courts of Justice; nor did the judges or Crown lawyers, whatever may have been their practice, venture to deny its legal authority. This fact must be borne in mind when we come to consider the contention of Catholic prisoners in these reigns as to their legal right to use equivocation as sanctioned by the Roman law. Since then this liberty has been excluded effectually from our courts, and no such contention can any longer be sustained either in law or conscience in English law courts.

When theologians explain the offices and

duties of the various classes of persons engaged in legal procedure, their method is first to explain the common law, and then the special law and custom of their own country. St. Alphonsus follows this plan; he first lays down the duty of a witness as determined by the civil law, and then speaks of the local custom of Naples, in which his lectures were delivered and first published. He does not speak of the English law, for it was no part of his duty or that of his hearers to know anything about it; but he lays down the principle that all just laws bind in conscience their own subjects, and that all legal decisions of the judge are no less binding.

The mind and habits of a nation are so deeply affected by the law daily administered before its eyes, and its very notions of moral rectitude are so coloured by it, and so widely divergent has the English law of procedure become from the Roman law, that Englishmen will mostly find a difficulty in seeing the wisdom and morality of the older system. I certainly do not admit that the English law holds up a higher standard of morality than the Roman law; I am convinced of the contrary, although

I believe each to be best suited to its own sphere. What I wish to insist on is that in the matters in question it is not Catholic theology, but the canon and Roman laws, explained with all sincerity by St. Alphonsus, that are upon their trial.

It remains for some future law historian to point out the profound change wrought by Christianity on the spirit of the Roman law as it was when Constantine was converted to the faith. The change most to our present purpose was that by which this first Christian Emperor, in compliance with the words of our Saviour, Matthew xviii., 16, "In the mouth of two or three witnesses let every word stand," decreed that in future no one was to be, not merely condemned, but even arraigned on the evidence of one witness only (C. iv., 20, 9), whence the maxim " *testis unus, testis nullus.*" The law of evidence and pleading was gradually perfected on the lines of Christian charity till the close of the *corpus juris civilis,* and had obtained its present form when the faculties of canon and civil law were established in the academies and universities of Europe, let us say, roughly, in the twelfth century.

In order to avoid misapprehension there is one peculiarity of the Roman law which must be borne in mind, namely, that a consensus of jurisconsults " made law," and is to be quoted as law. In this respect the *jus Romanum* differed from our law, because with us, not the opinions of jurists, but the decisions of judges acquiesced in by their brother judges, amount to a new determination of the law. The reason of the difference is—a matter much to the present point—that in the Roman system the judges were not necessarily trained jurists, and in consequence were naturally expected to be guided by their professional inferiors, while in our system the judges are the *élite* of the faculty, and by reason of their training as well as their office are best suited to interpret the law in new and undetermined contingencies. My reason for calling attention to this point is that, as I shall have to allege some points of Roman law in what follows, the reader may understand that I do not rely on the written codes, with which I am incompetent to deal, but on the *consensus juristarum*, which is an authoritative expression of the law, and practically the law itself.

The first point in the Roman law I wish to call attention to is this, that no criminal cause can be introduced *in forum*, that is by way of public accusation, until, in the first place, the judge is satisfied that there is a *semi-plena probatio* of the guilt of the accused, and that if one witness only of the fact can be produced the trial is to be quashed. There are exceptions to this rule—for instance, crimes pernicious to the community or State, such as conspiracy, treason, &c. In the next place, the law never obliges or wishes anyone to incriminate himself or another, except where the public good requires it, and in other cases the law allows the accused or witness to deny the charge, although true, unless the semiplene proof is made known to him, in which case he is bound to confess the truth.

There are certain exceptional cases in which the law obliges everyone cognisant of a crime to denounce it, and to give evidence of it whether in the preliminary examination or in the arraignment, even though he be the only witness of the fact. Generally, however, the law exempts a witness of the fact from giving evidence unless apart from him there is already a semiplene proof of guilt. Consequently, in cases of purely occult crime, with the exceptions stated, whether in the case of the accused or of the witness, or of anyone else, as may incidentally arise in the process of examination in court, the deponent not only can, but is bound to conceal the crime.

If under examination the witness is asked, either from inadvertence, ignorance, or malice, for any information the law exempts him from giving, such question is *praeter legem*, and no obligation to answer arises from it even though insisted upon by the judge. The reason of this is that he who swears in obedience to the law, is bound by his oath in the sense of the law, and no further. It is a maxim that the obligation of an oath is interpreted by the common law, and what the law allows to be withheld is not included in the oath. Therefore when a deponent swears " to tell the whole truth," the law lays down that the words are to be understood with the clause: "saving the law and the authority of the superior," whence the rule; " an oath is to be interpreted according to the mind of the legislator manifested by the common law." The words of the oath, " to tell the whole truth," have by special legal convention the tacit limitation "so far as I am legally bound." As a rule doubtless, and always in matters of opinion, the deponent is bound to take the ruling of the judge as the right interpretation of the law; but if it is clear and certain to him that the law allows him to withhold a point of evidence, then the Roman and canon laws further allow him by amphibology to baffle the illegal inquisition. These are some of the conclusions of the two common laws; they are based on the law of charity and justice, and are intended to secure all who cannot be proved criminals from useless defamation, or innocent persons from unwarranted condemnation; they rely on the sanctity of an oath and on the reverence Christians have for it, and bear testimony to the desire of the law to rescue deponents placed in exceptionally difficult circumstances from the temptation to commit perjury.

What I have said on this matter I have taken from ecclesiastical jurists, mostly Doctors *in utroque jure,* but I have examined the *jus scriptum,* so far as I thought required to feel myself on safe ground. The question will be found treated in the commentaries on the second book of the decretals of Gregory IX. t.t., vii., xviii., xx., xxiv. The references as given by the commentators on these titles will introduce the reader who wishes to pursue the matter further to the full exposition of both laws as given by the older writers. There cannot, I should hope, be much difficulty in gathering from the foregoing the meaning of St. Alphonsus and other moral writers when laying down the duties of deponents in courts of law. They are simply instructing the subjects of those laws in their duties and privileges as laid down by the law itself. It is a mere superstition to suppose that an oath binds beyond the thoroughly understood and express convention between him who swears and him who receives the oath, and in courts of law the two parties concerned are the deponent and the law itself; of which the judge, so long as he acts legally, is the impersonation. Such, at least, is the convention according to the laws of which theologians speak, and it has not yet been shown that even the English law has renounced convention, or will regard a deponent who has in all things answered according to law, as a perjurer.

There is, as I have said, an uncommon difference between the spirit and special determinations of the English law and the common laws of which I have been speaking; and I have said that according to Catholic theology the particular law of any country is that which has before all others to be obeyed. But although the determinations are so different, the principle for which I am contending, namely, the legality of equivocation in a court of justice, whether with or without an oath, is admitted and acted upon in our English courts.

For example, the accused is allowed to plead " not guilty," although in reality he is guilty of the act laid to his charge, and no one, I think, but a fanatic will condemn him for doing so. The English law, while it insists on an answer, allows the answer to be in such a form that he who uses it can hide his crime, and this by a phrase that obviously and with semblance of truth denies the commission of the crime. An innocent man uses it in this sense; a guilty man uses it in another—yet a lawful sense.

Again, it is common to all law that witnesses should swear to " tell the whole truth," and all law acknowledges an unexpressed restriction on the obvious meaning of the words. In the Roman and canon laws they are understood with the restriction, "So far as I am questioned," and, "So far as I am legally bound to depose," and the oath itself binds in this sense only. In English law the obligation of the oath is also restricted by privileged cases. The witness is not bound to answer questions, for instance, incriminating himself, but if he chooses to answer, his reply is understood to be covered by the oath. Anyhow, in the case supposed he may refuse to answer, notwithstanding his oath to "tell the whole truth," and no one will say that the restriction used is unlawful. In fact, as in all cases the witness is bound to swear " to the mind of the law," so in every law some mental restriction is legalized, as if by necessity.

A witness in a court of law discharges a duty honourable in itself and highly important to the well-being of the State. In the Roman and canon law it is, moreover, a sacred duty—begun with a solemn act of worship and a profession of Faith—for an oath is such. As a rule, these laws desire that persons of good repute only should be admitted to depose, that they should be treated with reverence and confidence, and that much should be left to their conscience, for they are presumed to be truthful, loyal, and willing to promote the ends of justice. The duties of a witness, therefore, become an important part of the religious education of every Christian citizen. No doubt the Anglican clergy, though they may not have reached this conception of the office of a witness, nevertheless explain to their hearers the obligations of an oath, and unless they choose to allow the sacred act to become a snare for perjury, they will point out that oaths are to be interpreted not arbitrarily, but by authenticated rules, and that their obligations are to be sometimes limited by what Catholic jurists speak of as mental restriction, but what in the English sense is more aptly designated legal convention.

The principle, then, that equivocation or mental restriction—in the sense in which these words are used in theology, though not in the vulgar sense—is recognized by English law and practised in its Courts (though to a limited extent) will not be denied by any honest controversialist. This common principle of all laws being admitted, it remains to be seen in what respects there is a declared divergence between the English law and the common law in their respective applications of this principle. I have said, and I cannot lay too much stress on the fact, that by all theology the law of one's country and not the common law where the two happen to diverge, is that which binds in conscience. All, no matter what be their nationality, who appear in a court of justice where English law is administered, are bound by the law of that court, not only exteriorly but in conscience, whatever any other law may determine, if only the law of the court is a just law.

I have put this last limitation expressly, because there is one point, perhaps—I may safely say one only—in which, according to theology, the English law of evidence is unjust, and cannot be obeyed in conscience. This is the case of a priest, who, through confession, or through what is known as a secret of counsel confided to him in character of his sacred office, knows a fact, the revelation of which may bring any detriment, however small, to another. Here secrecy is a Divine law, which no human law can abrogate, no oath can prevail against. A priest who expects to be examined on such a matter, and is compelled by the law to swear to tell the whole truth, should, if he cannot avoid taking the oath, take it under an express restriction, "saving my order," or other words to the same effect, take the required oath, but with or without express restriction, every oath is limited by the clause *salvo jure divino,* not because this is laid down in the common law, but because by the natural law, the second condition of an oath *justitia,* renders it impossible that an injustice or an impiety can be covered by the oath.

In two respects the English and Roman laws are strikingly contrasted: the first is the estimate they exhibit of the sanctity of an oath; the other, the value they set on private rights, with respect to reputation, or, as we say, to a good name. In the Roman system there is great caution observed not only in the selection of witnesses, but also in making known the exact duties imposed on a witness by his oath, in order to exclude, as far as human prudence can, the crime of perjury. In the English system the sacredness of an oath is merely legal, and much the same as a solemn declaration. The witness has to look to himself, and see that he is not caught tripping by an expert cross-examiner. Again, according to the Roman system, the revelation of private wrong-doing, except so far as is necessary for the vindication of justice, is discountenanced, and the accused and witnesses are protected from useless or malicious exposure. The practice of the English courts does not exhibit the same degree of humanity. With these remarks I can return to the last extract taken from Dr. Littledale's letter, p. 72.

I must count the misrepresentations in that extract. 1. The instances given of the teaching of St. Alphonsus have no connection whatever with the "exception" which they are said to make insecure. The "exception" refers exclusively to the just cause in taking an oath, or to the necessity for it, the instances subjoined by Dr. Littledale, suppose a just cause, and refer to the interpretation only of the oath. 2. Pope Innocent never tried to make prohibited mental reservation, for he was a wise and learned man, and knew that he could not reverse the law of Nature. He condemned, and very effectually, "reservation purely mental," as may be seen from the propositions he condemned, as they are given by St. Alphonsus (*l.c.*). The unanimous interpretation of approved canonists and jurists who wrote after the decree shows clearly enough what Innocent meant to condemn, and no approved writer has ever questioned his wisdom or presumed to contravene his precept. 3. There are misrepresentations in the words "vainly tried," because, first, the Pope did not try to do what is imputed to him; next, he perfectly succeeded in achieving what he undertook to do. 4. St. Alphonsus does not speak of a witness "irregularly questioned," but of one illegally questioned on a point the secresy of which is provided for by law. When the question itself is legal, and the court qualified to put it, the oath always binds to the disclosure asked for, notwithstanding mere irregularity in the questioning. 5. Such a witness, as St. Alphonsus contemplates, and no other, may swear that he "does not know the crime . . . though, in truth, he knows it, meaning that he does not know it so as to be legally questioned as to it, or to depose to it." This is the convention and instruction given by the civil and canon law, through their recognized interpreters, to the accused and witnesses. The accuser of St. Alphonsus should begin by showing that it is beyond the power of law to make such convention. 6. Dr. Littledale proceeds, "And if the act be one which the witness himself does not consider a crime, &c." The words of St. Alphonsus are, "And if the witness, upon another count, is not bound to depose, for instance, if it is evident to him that the crime was without fault, &c." The reader will have no difficulty in detecting the unfairness of Dr. Littledale's words. First, there is the suppression of the words limiting the case to a legal privilege of reticence; next, the words "*si ipsi constat*" are not correctly translated, as "does not himself *consider;*" but the translation fits in conveniently with what went before about "what are *considered* adequate reasons." The insinuation of Dr. Littledale in both these unwarrantable expressions is that St. Alphonsus allows the witness to act on his own opinions as to what is and what is not criminal, whereas the saint is speaking only of what is laid down in the law. 7. The case spoken of by St. Alphonsus is about as well known to jurists as estimating a personal equation is known to astronomers, and is equally an enigma to untrained sciolists. It is this: there are certain acts which in law are presumed to be criminal until a just cause is proved, such, for instance, as homicide. A witness knows that the accused committed the act of homicide, but he knows also (*sibi constat*) that it was done purely in self-defence, and without using any unnecessary violence. He knows therefore that, *in the eye of the law*, the accused is not guilty. But the case so stands that his evidence to the fact will oblige the judge to condemn the accused, by the application of a legal presumption not verified in the case, and that consequently his evidence will lead to the condemnation to death of a man innocent morally, and *in the eye of the law*. In this case the law itself wishes him to suppress the fact, and authorizes him to do so by means of an equivocation. This is the case referred to by St. Alphonsus, as may easily be gathered from the authors to whom he sends us for further information. 8. Dr. Littledale illustrates the teaching of St. Alphonsus by the " example " of " agrarian murder in

Ireland." The example is unwarranted, for the Saint is not speaking of English law but of Roman law, nor is there any room for inference from one to the other. 9. And it is again unwarrantable because the Saint only speaks of acts not culpable in the eye of the law; wilful murder is culpable in all law.

4. I have already pointed out that the Roman law does not, unless in exceptional cases, allow the occult crime of an accused man to be deposed to in court unless there is semi-plene evidence apart from that of the witness in question, and that it allows the remedy of equivocation in order to conceal the crime. Dr. Littledale applies this to English law, of which the Saint says nothing, and in which different rules for obtaining evidence are in force.

5. He attributes to St. Alphonsus the teaching that "Those who have thus sworn falsely are entitled to absolution, &c." St. Alphonsus declares that, "Those who have thus sworn" have not sworn falsely, but truly, and lawfully; and, as he knew nothing of High Church practices, we are not to be surprised that he has not a word about absolving imaginary perjurers, or obliging them to reveal

a fact that the law forbids them to reveal. It ought, however, to be a matter of surprise that so earnest an advocate of truth as this writer claims to be, should have omitted all reference to the following words of St. Alphonsus, which immediately follow the last case given, and furnish not only a rule for judging of his whole doctrine on " the matters at issue," but also on the cases ingeniously imported into them by his accuser. The words are, "The accused, however, or witness, who is legally questioned by the judge, cannot use any equivocation, because he is bound by the just precept of his superiors."

In the Roman courts the judge himself conducted the examination, and the accused was the principal person examined. This explains the way in which St. Alphonsus speaks, and indicates the law which he explains. But the moral principles which guide his conclusions show as clear as noonday that he condemns, as every theologian will condemn, the practice which his accuser gives as examples of what he allows.

Dr. Littledale proceeds: " Further, it is lawful to suborn perjured evidence ' if you have a great interest in employing perjury to expose the fraud of another person in order to obtain your own rights.' ("Theol. Moral.," iii., 77)." This is, indeed, bold, and looks almost as if this writer were courting a Nemesis for the endless slanders he loves to utter against Catholic teaching. The answer, however, to this infamous untruth is as follows:—In the Roman law a convicted perjurer could never again be admitted to an oath on the legal presumption, "once a liar, always a liar." A man once convicted of bearing false witness became "infamous," and the rule was, not only in courts but in common converse, "*amandandus sit.*" There were, however, some exceptions as to swearing a perjurer, and hence the question of St. Alphonsus—"Is it lawful to ask a perjurer to swear?" and as the answer is that in two cases it is lawful, Dr. Littledale translates the question into the proposition, "*It is lawful to suborn perjured evidence.*"

In the text commented upon by St. Alphonsus, this question first appears in the treatise on perjury, from which Dr. Littledale has up to this been misquoting. It occurs L. iv., n. 146, and is put as follows:—"He also sins grievously who exacts an oath from another, knowing him to be a perjurer, unless a just cause and necessity require it; because then (in such exceptional case), the perjury proceeds solely from the malice of the perjurer, nor is the other (who exacts it) considered morally its cause, since he uses his right." St. Alphonsus refers us back to the third book, where he explains this point under the treatise of charity, and in the chapter on material co-operation in the sin of another. He explains, n. 63, the difference between "formal co-operation" in the sin of another, and "material co-operation." The former is that "which concurs with the evil *will* of another, and which cannot be without sin." Concurrence with the will of another, as generally explained, is by consent, counsel, mandate (employment), request, &c. Concurrence in any of these ways with the sin of another, and consequently with perjury, is intrinsically wrong, is that "which cannot be without sin;" and therefore in no conceivable circumstances, according to St. Alphonsus and all approved writers, can suborning or employing perjured evidence be lawful.

St. Alphonsus then explains "material co-operation," which is concurrence in the evil act only of another without intention. This kind of co-operation (material) may according to the circumstances be lawful or unlawful. For its lawfulness those conditions were required which I enumerated at the beginning of this paper, p. 40, and it is only necessary to repeat here that the act of him who co-operates (calls on a perjurer to swear) must be lawful in itself, that the act called for must be separable from all sin, that the sin foreseen is attributable solely to the malice of the other, and in no way influenced by the co-operator, and that there must be a just cause for material co-operation. St. Alphonsus explains all this, n.n. 59-62, and adds: "When you do an action which is indifferent (not unlawful) without a wrong intention, if the other wishes to abuse it, in order to commit his sin, you are not bound except by charity to prevent him, &c." Having put this explanation before the theological student, he inquires "Whether it is lawful to ask an oath of a perjurer?" He answers that, "under proper conditions, it is lawful in two cases—first, when a judge has to do so *ex-officio;* next, when it is important to your interests to use the perjury in order to make clear the frauds of the other (*alterius*, the perjurer; possibly, 'of another'), that you may obtain your right." This, too, is a case examined by scores of jurists and theologians, of whose meaning there can be no shadow of doubt. We have an instance in the case of Daniel, who forced the elders to swear to their charges against Susannah, that he might save a holy and innocent woman from a shameful death, and of St. Athanasius, who, at the Council of Tyre, forced his accuser to swear to a calumny in order that he might vindicate his own good name. St. Alphonsus never says a word to justify the base accusation that he allowed " suborning " or " employing " perjured evidence.

Having demolished St. Alphonsus so effectually, Dr. Littledale next turns his attention to the Jesuits. "And as to the doctrine that the end justifies the means," he continues, " it is the received maxim of the principal Jesuit writers on moral theology. I will only cite Busembaum, &c." And to prove this rather threadbare calumny he quotes from Busembaum the words, " When the end is lawful the means also are lawful," and this he thinks is sufficient evidence for the accusation. The reference given to Busembaum is perfectly useless, but if the proper reference had been given I have no doubt we could easily see by the context, and the comment of St. Alphonsus, what the author meant by the words ascribed to him. I have explained above the only theological sense in which the words can be understood; it is probably a legal form, meaning that the law desires all to have lawful means to secure their rights. Again, undoubtedly Busembaum speaks of a definite end and definite means, and lets his readers know that such means are lawful for that end; anyhow, we should know of what means he speaks, for unless he speaks of means wrong of themselves, his words prove nothing. All I can say is this, as I have been unable to find the place referred to by Dr. Littledale, and have a very decided view as to the value of his evidence, and a certain confidence in my own knowledge of theology, I am prepared to stake all I have in the world that Busembaum nowhere favours the doctrine his accuser imputes to him.

Dr. Littledale's line of argument, or that which he gives us as such, is well worthy of analysis for one who has an interest in detecting fraudulent evidence, and ascertaining the "notes" thereof. In the first paragraph of his letter he gives us to understand that by the "principle," or "doctrine," or "maxim," that "the end justifies the means," is signified that "it is lawful to do evil for a good end," "to break a lawful oath or to tell a lie, or to do any other wicked thing whatsoever for the sake of promotion of the supposed interests of the Church," &c. In the next paragraph he goes on to say that such teaching as this, " the Roman Catholic Church has as nearly as possible affirmed." This accusation is made in answer to a categorical repudiation of such teaching on the part of Catholics, which repudiation the accuser characterizes as being ." in direct opposition to indisputable facts." Here at least is a plain issue, a horrible accusation brought on one side, a flat denial on the other. The burden of proof rests with the accuser; the accused is to be judged innocent till the crime laid against him is proved. The accuser is an Anglican High Church clergyman, the accused (to put the matter in the concrete) the Catholic clergy of England and Ireland. The moral analyst will keep an eye on the character of the opponents, chiefly as to their truthfulness, and as to the motive of the accusation; but of all this later.

For the present he will have to examine the evidence which has been placed before him in confirmation of so grave a charge, and the manner in which it has been "got up." If he has patience he will count the mistranslations, misstatements, and downright untruths with which it is interspersed, and when he has separated the small residuum of truth it contains, he will ask himself, What has this to do with the accusation? But the accused, we Catholics, are not satisfied with merely challenging the proof of the accusation against us. We do not stand on the ground that the case against us is " not proven; " we say the evidence is concocted, dishonest, and simply villainous. The charge against us is atrocious, and well merits these epithets, and we undertake to show that the direct contrary to all we are charged with is the unmistakable teaching of our Church and of our theology. This I think I have already shown, not as fully as might be, but yet sufficiently; my present duty is to examine the adverse evidence.

What is called the "doctrine" that "the end justifies the means," is explained in the first paragraph of Dr. Littledale's letter to mean that wrong may be done for a good end, such as to tell a lie, or break a lawful oath. A Catholic who declares himself a convert repudiates this doctrine in the name of all Catholics, and declares it detestable. Dr. L. desires to correct the statement. The Catholic, he tells the British public, like most converts, is unfamiliar with the system he has adopted; the Doctor himself knows all about it, but "Rome's recruits" are to be put out of court as incompetent witnesses. Again, Catholic priests, like myself, who are not converts, are not to be listened to. Is not the avowed object of Dr. Littledale's labours to show that we are deceivers, and not to be trusted? It is true he undertakes to prove both the ignorance of converts and the dishonesty of Catholic priests by first establishing the "doctrine" in question, and he establishes the doctrine by putting out of court every competent witness except the accusers; but after what we have seen of the character of his evidence *in re* Liguori, it would be superfluous to charge him with *petitio principii*, or with poisoning the wells. Anyhow, he shall have a fair hearing, nor will I urge that he is a witness " not above exception."

His allegation then is that it is a "maxim,"and a " doctrine " of the principal Jesuit writers that " the end justifies the means," in the sense explained. We have first to see what he says as to the existence of the maxim, " the received maxim ; " its meaning is a distinct question. A maxim is a form of words with a declared meaning. The form, " the end justifies the means," is attributed to Jesuit writers, notwithstanding repeated denials. Dr. L. has the whole Court to himself, and hundreds of Jesuit writers to produce. If they have such a maxim it must be somewhere in their books, and a " maxim " common to numerous writers must frequently occur. To prove against any writer a "maxim," it should be found in his writings, or at least in his verbal explanations, *totidem verbis*. Here I do not ask for more verbal accuracy, although I might claim it. I only claim that the allegation be sustained by the production of some formula meaning that wrong can ever be done for any end whatsoever. Where, I ask, in Jesuit writers is there a formula or maxim implying this? None such is produced; for the excellent reason, that none such has ever been written. The question is as to whether Jesuit writers use certain words as a "maxim." Yes, says their accuser, but he only says yes; he does not and cannot produce a single example.

Dr. L. is under examination, and the questions and answers may be conceived as follows, they seem to fit his case :—Q. : You state that this is a received maxim of Jesuit writers. Please favour us with an example of the maxim from their writings.—A. : Well, really I cannot at present recall any example, but there is another maxim.— Q. : We are not at present concerned with another maxim. If you have no example of this maxim to produce, why do you attribute it to those writers?—A. : I am sure they meant it, and I can prove— Q. : We do not want your opinions or your inference at the present stage of the examination. If you cannot produce any instance of a Jesuit writer using the words in question, why do you impute to so many of them the maxim itself?—No answer.—Q. : Well, let us come to the other maxim, what is it?—A.: Well, Busembaum says that when the end is lawful the means also are lawful.—Q.: What is the meaning of that?—A.: Oh, it can only mean that the end justifies the means. —Q.: Please point out the grounds of this inference of yours.—A.: Don't you perceive that when a Jesuit says that the " means are lawful," he can only mean that they are " wrong."—Q.: Well, as that is not self-evident, what reason have you for saying that those writers, when they speak of " lawful means," are to be understood as meaning " wrong means?"—A.: Because this is their " received maxim," as I have said.—Q.: What maxim are you speaking of?—A.: That the end justifies the means.—Q.: Are you aware that they and all Catholics deny that there is any such maxim, and have asked in vain for a single example of it?—A.: Of course they do, but they are all either ignorant of the Popish system or not to be trusted.—Q.: But what proof do you bring of so serious a charge?— A.: The maxim itself, which is an indisputable fact.—Q.: What motive have you in bringing forward this abominable charge?—A.: The whole thing is explained in the third section of my penny tract, entitled "The Claims of Rome."—Q.: Please explain further.—A.: Well, you see that there are a great number of our disciples whom we speak of as "hankerers after Rome," and who are beginning to have misgivings as to our apostolate, and are asking whether we are really priests or Catholics, or only pretenders. Many of them have already left us, and more are on the way to join the recruits. The situation is awkward; and as the end justifies the means, we must have some means of securing these infatuated hankerers from having any intercourse with Catholic priests. The means we have adopted are to throw discredit on the truthfulness of Catholic priests; these are the only resource left us, and we at least hold that our end is good.

The principle that the end justifies the means, formerly known by its correlative expression of doing evil for a good end, has always been in abhorrence among Catholics. They were accused of this at the time of the Apostles, and no doubt the whole class of polemists who covered licentiousness with verbal rigidity, reproduced the charge. The Jansenists and their *protégés* of the new-born Anglican Church accused the Jesuits of acting on this principle, because the latter taught some things to be lawful which the former denounced as wrong, such, for instance, as the use of probabilism and epieikeia. The sophism was telling, and soon passed from the hands of the clever and learned Jansenists into those of their less favoured allies in England and Germany, men who had not been trained in the schools and knew little of scholastic terminology. It was embodied in the form of a maxim, expressive of what Protestants wished to fasten on the Jesuits, and the latest development is to attribute the maxim itself to them. It sounds neat enough to the uneducated ear, but when we come to analyze its meaning, we discern that no system of Catholic philosophy or theology can have produced it, and it stands condemned by intrinsic evidence as an invention of the enemy. See p. 16.

But yet we have the formula, as Dr. Littledale translates it, "when the end is lawful, the means also are lawful." I do not complain of the translation, for the original is ambiguous; nevertheless, I think think the words "*etiam licent media*" are properly rendered, "there are also lawful means." But the difference is not important. I have already explained that the only significations admissible in the formula, are either that the special means indicated in the context are on their own consideration lawful, or else that the law intends that where there is a right there should be some lawful means of securing it. While writing this, I have come across a legal judgment pronounced some years ago in the House of Lords, in conformity with a report of the English judges, and lately quoted as an authority by Chief Baron Palles, in which the maxim is quoted, "*quando aliquid mandatur, mandatur et omne per quod perveniatur ad illud*" ("Times," January 6, 1887), which means "when any work is committed to another, all the means for its attainment are appointed." This surely cannot signify that unlawful means are appointed for carrying out the mandate of the law. Yet, "*omne per quod perveniatur,*" is a much wider expression than "*media licita.*"

I think any sensible person would at once see the meaning of the legal maxim, even though he had nothing but the formula itself to guide him; but in this case the context explains it. The question was whether it was lawful or obligatory on the part of the constabulary police in Ireland to give active aid to bailiffs in the serving of writs. The judgment was in the affirmative, and the maxim was quoted as embodying the reasons for it. In the same way if Dr. L., in place of giving a perfectly useless reference to Busembaum to the pages of one of the two hundred editions of the work, had quoted—as he was bound—the book and chapter of the author, we could say more exactly what the words quoted signify, as well from the context as from the commentators, chiefly St. Alphonsus, who explain the condensed matter of Busembaum.

A maxim, whether in philosophy, law, or theology, is sometimes a paradox, sometimes a fiction, sometimes a metaphor, but always needs careful explanation to be rightly understood. I suppose most people remember the fun which students of physics from Galileo to almost our own time made of the saying "Nature abhors a vacuum," and yet this saying signifies one of the most important truths in natural physics, if only it be rightly understood. In common conversation there is a saying " Where there is a will there is a way," and we know what this means when spoken by an honest man, although a rogue may use it in a bad sense. Again, "All is pure to the pure." This has a Christian sense, the true sense of the maxim, but it also has its Lutheran sense. In fine, all these maxims have their right and proper signification, but are open to an evil construction at the hands of the malicious.

There are some minds, or perhaps I should say some characters, who can only account by the suggestion of evil for what is above their intelligence in the words and actions of their neighbours. Let anyone observe in times of political excitement the language which partisans address to great and high-minded statesmen who are opposed to them. We have lately seen that the life of a man like Father Damien has been characterized as one of diabolical wickedness by men who could only have known that he was a priest, and had devoted his life to the service of the forlorn and afflicted. Fortunately the world itself is turning away from such brutality, and I trust also it is beginning to understand the meaner malice of imputing evil meaning to a harmless form of words.

We had hoped that this senseless style of controversy had met with its death-blow some years back at the hands of Cardinal Newman. No one who has read his description of the Anglophobe Russian General can forget the arguments drawn by the General from English maxims of law, such as "the king can do no wrong," and "Parliament is omnipotent." It would be amusing to observe how an Englishman would set about disabusing a foreigner of extravagant notions regarding these maxims. Undoubtedly the best way of dealing with an obstinate opponent of this stamp is satire. If you cannot instruct him let the world see that he is making a fool of himself, lest he should befool others. But there is another way of speaking to a man who wants to know the truth, and this I venture to adopt lest I should leave incomplete what I have undertaken to explain.

An ethical or legal maxim is a symbol standing for a whole group of practical truths which cannot be collected under a single definition, nor adequately expressed by any one form of words. It is useful in currency as a measure and guide in conduct, but cannot be well explained in the abstract, and can never be the *premiss* of a syllogism. Nothing can be proved from it in strict logic; it can only be itself ascertained by a learner seeing how it is applied in particular cases.

Yet there is a general notion of the meaning of a maxim in any community in which it is more or less current; though this regards rather what it does not comprehend than what it does. Every Englishman knows that the King can do wrong, and that the maxim has no reference to his moral being, in any sense; but we do not generally know whether the King is amenable to courts of justice for debt, libel, or assault. This any good lawyer can tell us. Now the patent absurdity of attributing moral immunity to any human being, and the persuasion universal in the community that the maxim does not imply any such immunity, are sufficient reasons to convince any sensible foreigner of the truth, and if he refuses to be convinced by this he must be regarded either as intellectually incompetent to form a sound opinion, or a rogue who wishes to foment discord.

This notwithstanding, an inquirer may honestly say, So far the proof is good, but there is a yet more authentic proof wanted.

It is not an idle maxim floating about the community or confined to law books. Many high authorities who have written on the constitution must have somehow explained it; statesmen in Parliament must have quoted it; and above all the high legal authorities of the land must have decided many cases according to its sense. Show from these sources also that it does not touch the question of moral responsibility, and I will admit that you have proved your case in every possible way.

The maxim "The king can do no wrong" is a paradox, and if challenged by a controversialist, calls for explanation, but everyone knows where to find the maxim and to look for its explanation. It is of the essence of a maxim belonging to any code, that it be expressly set forth, that it have its recognized interpretation, and its assigned place in the system to which it belongs. But the alleged maxim, "The end justifies the means," and its equivalent, "It is lawful to do evil for a good end," are neither truisms nor paradoxes. They are simply an enormity; they are nowhere found in our writers, nor heard of in our schools, nor implied in our conclusions. They are simply unknown to theology, and are therefore nowhere explained by it. Whence do they come—alien in verbal form to the language of all the ecclesiastical schools, legal as well as theological, and abhorrent to our spirit? They are simply the work of "an enemy," who has sown them among our good seed that he may bring discredit on the labourers in the field. But the maxim " Where the end is lawful the means also are lawful," though no paradox, may be admitted to be ambiguous. Let me suppose, for the sake of clearness, that it includes materially the meaning—which, however, I deny it to have—that unlawful means can ever be regarded as lawful because of a good end. The question is whether this meaning is intended or excluded in the sense in which the maxim is used; as, in the other maxim, whether moral immunity is intended or not in the person of the King.

That the alleged sense is excluded in theology from the maxim as to the means and the end is proved in every possible way. First, as to the community in general, every Catholic knows, for he has been taught so from his first catechism upwards, that it is never lawful to do wrong, such as to tell a lie even to save the whole world. Next, all preachers who are the legitimate expounders of the laws of the Church and stand in the same place as Jurists in civil law, give the same evidence. Thirdly, all expounders of the moral law, from the earliest fathers of the Church down to the latest approved writer, speak to the same effect. Fourthly, I have taken Dr. Littledale's word that there is such a maxim as he quotes, but I cannot remember to have ever come across it. I cannot, therefore, say that I have seen any explanation regarding it, but I know that the sense Dr. Littledale puts upon it is expressly excluded by every theologian whom I have consulted, certainly not less than fifty. I fully admit that I have met with some solutions in the writings of theologians, namely, the Summists, which appeared to me to involve that principle—I always thought unconsciously to the author—but I have never seen any such solution that was not upon its publication condemned by the Holy See. There is an example to the point in the condemnation of the opinion regarding purely mental restriction.

To complete my proof, I come to the judicial pronouncements of the Church bearing on the subject. We have some hundreds of propositions taken from various writers and condemned by the Holy See, which, extracted from the various decrees in which they were condemned, are generally given in a compendious form at the beginning of their course by later moral theologians. They are also to be found in Denzinger's "Enchiridion," and in other collections of the Acts of the Holy See. These condemned propositions deal to a great extent with moral questions, and repeatedly we find among them opinions that what is wrong may be allowed in order to preserve life or honour, or for some other necessity; not that the authors held that the acts were wrong and could be justified, but, as we must believe, they erroneously thought them to be indifferent. All such opinions are condemned, and forbidden to be taught, held, or acted upon. So that we may take it as a rule in the tribunals of the Church, by which propositions touching on all moral *questions* are judged, that no proposition will be tolerated which implies the lawfulness of any act which is wrong in itself, whatever be its end or necessity.

I do not reproduce these judicial decisions

here, for I have no space for such a purpose, and many of them would be unsuitable for reproduction in a work like this. But the reader can find them with a little trouble if he chooses to consult the general references I have given, and he will find in them not only what I have undertaken to prove, but also the exquisite care and pastoral solicitude of the Holy See to preserve Catholic theology in its purity and guard it from all that might mar it or expose it to just reproach. Let him who suspects this theology of any laxity or carelessness on the subject of the end justifying the means, look over the thousands of cases solved by St. Alphonsus and other casuists, and if he can point out one proposition that truly involves the "detestable principle" in question, I will guarantee that such proposition shall be condemned within a twelvemonth by the highest tribunal of the Church.*

* Since writing the above, I have found the passage in which Busembaum says: "To whom the end is lawful, the means also are lawful" (L. vi., vi., 1). It is as I have said. Busembaum is speaking of means of their own nature honest, and indicated by the natural law as the fit means of a lawful end, but which are not allowed unless in certain circumstances. The question regards the conjugal state, in which the end and the means are legalised by the circumstance of wedlock. If the end is admitted to be lawful, the lawfulness of the fit means can be proved from it, and *vice-versâ*. In this, as in similar questions, theologians say that the circumstances, in-

Everyone who accepts the office of teaching in the sacred faculties is bound each year to swear solemnly to the creed of Pius IV., by which he binds himself *inter alia* never to interpret the holy Scriptures except according to the unanimous interpretation of the Fathers. Here I am met by Dr. Littledale, who says we teach that it is lawful for a good end to break a lawful oath. I shall return to this point shortly; at present I merely wish to point out the measures the Church has taken to secure unity and publicity of teaching in all matters of faith and morals. To confine myself to the faculty of moral theology, although there have been different schools of thought, and, as to its method, object, and special conclusions very great diversity, there never has been among Catholics the slightest diversity as to its main principles, nor would such ever have been tolerated.

That evil may be done for a good end, that a lie may be told or a lawful oath broken is expressly forbidden in Sacred Scripture, accord-

cluding the end, *cohonestant actum;* that is, add the required extrinsic legality to an act of its own nature honest and good. Surely, this is very different from justifying a wrong or evil act, the meaning which Dr. Littledale unwarrantably attaches to Busembaum's words. This also is the sense given to them by St. Alphonsus (*l.c.*, 934).

ing to the unanimous interpretation of the Fathers. A teacher of theology, then, apart from his denial of revealed truth, would also perjure himself if he were to teach any of these opinions, and this alone is enough to account for the absolute unanimity of all Catholic schools on these points. But these schools have had on other points prolonged and acrimonious disputes. The *odium theologicum*, the forgetfulness of charity, and the exaggerated imputations hurled about from school to school, have passed into a proverb, and frequently provoked the interference of the Holy See for their suppression. They are deeply to be regretted, but regrettable as they were, they sharpened the eyes and wits of clever and learned men to find some flaw in their opponent's armour. The watchword of all alike was the preservation of theology from all taint of error. Is it likely that a fundamental principle of morality such as any of those I have named could be undermined and endangered without creating an outburst of indignation?

Busembaum taught about the middle of the seventeenth century. His work was made known throughout Europe with an unprecedented rapidity. It was at a time when theological controversy was at its height in the schools, and when watchful and not friendly eyes were fixed on the writings and practice of Jesuits. Yet who among his Catholic opponents saw in his maxims anything subversive of Christian morality? Not one, I believe, for all knew these expressed theological truths, admitted by all, and that what he taught was honestly spoken. And yet we must suppose they knew quite as much of theology, and of the significance of its terms, as his later Protestant accusers. It would have been impossible for the Jesuits, even if they had desired it, to introduce an alien or suspected opinion into the schools without instant reclamation on the part of those who themselves stood on the ground of orthodox teaching.

Dr. Littledale closes his letter to the "Pall Mall" with the following remark, intended, no doubt, as the forensic conclusion of his remarkable evidence: "When it is borne in mind that no cause would seem more just, no end more lawful, to a Roman Catholic priest than making a proselyte, the above facts make excusable the conviction that minute scrupulousness about accuracy or about means is not to be looked for when a case of this sort is on hand." We can hardly catch the whole meaning of these words without comparing them with the last sentence of paragraph iii. of "The Claims of the Church of Rome," of which this letter is a mere reproduction, though prepared for a very different class of readers. It is as follows: "When, then, it is remembered that no cause would seem so just to a Roman Catholic zealot as winning a convert to his Church, it follows that unless we have some warrant that he does not accept Liguori's system, there is, at least, a risk that some inconvenient truth will be kept back, and convenient misstatements made, in order to smooth over any difficulties. And, in point of fact, such is actually the case."

Here we have the accusation brought out more clearly, and some light on the author's insinuations somewhat obscurely put forward in the letter as to " secresy " and " more than secresy " in the dealing of priests with converts, and their general ignorance of the " system " they adopt. I propose first speaking of the statement of this accuser as to us Catholic priests, that we sometimes endeavour to keep, sometimes actually do keep, persons who apply to us for instructions in the Catholic faith, in the dark in some respects, either as to our doctrine or practice. I will then give my opinion as to the conduct of the accuser.

I know as a fact that many Anglican and Nonconformist clergymen speak of Catholic priests as systematic liars, and teach their hearers that there are certain occult doctrines or practices among us which are carefully guarded from the public at large, and expressly from new converts. These later in course of time may be more fully informed, and then they will find themselves committed to a "system" from which they cannot withdraw, but which they would have died rather than embrace had they known it beforehand. This is the keynote of the lectures delivered by the stream of impostors in the pay of the Dublin Priests' Protection and other Protestant Societies; it is put forward more cautiously by Protestant clergymen, as I have said, and is clearly insinuated by Dr. Littledale.

It is not pleasant to deal with a charge of this nature, on account of its very foulness, but it is right that it should be clearly stated and receive such a disproof as it is capable of. Supposing that this was the dream of a morbid imagination, or the invention of an interested partisan, how could it be disproved? The only way could be, first, to examine the evidence in support of the charge; next, the character of the witnesses brought to support it and their motive; then, as positive rebutting evidence is impossible, negative evidence may be produced, the absurdity of the charge shown, and the character of the accused brought to light. This plan of disproval I propose to follow.

The direct evidence is exclusively the "experiences" of a class of lecturers who, claiming to be Catholic priests converted to Anglicanism, or escaped nuns, reveal the awful things they pretend to have witnessed while in the house of bondage. As the antecedents of such persons are generally well known to the police, and many of their acts recorded in the courts of justice, it is not a difficult thing to trace their career, and to show the impossibility of their being witnesses of the facts they testify to. This cannot be done in all cases, for the name of this class of witnesses is legion, but it has been done in many cases, notably in those of Achilli, Maria

Monk, and Dr. Keatinge. As often as their evidence is sufficiently definite as to time, persons, and places, it has been brought to the test, and as often as tested has been proved to be an imposture. No single fact of any importance in our present question has ever been successfully sustained by them, or brought to proof, and the residuum of generalities they utter is no more worthy of credit than their evidence.

It will be hardly necessary for me to say much of the character or credibility of those witnesses. They are now pretty well understood in all except the lower strata of English society. We no longer see archbishops or bishops presiding at their lectures, and the clergy trooping to gain edification from their denunciations of Rome. But one, at least, of the Protestant societies keeps them in hand and pays them handsomely. That society is not particular as to credentials, certificates, &c. It does not make awkward inquiries as to antecedents, nor look for information except in unembarrassing quarters. A well-spiced story with a poisoning case or two, and a few thrilling adventures, will be enough to make the executive committee believe the account, and if the applicant for the Protestant apostolate has sufficient address to face an audience, he is pretty sure to have two pounds a week and perquisites so long as he keeps out of the hands of the police. The procedure shows at once the character and motive of this class of witnesses.

Stories of the same kind come to us in another way, that is without any witnesses or evidence at all other than "it is said," or "believed by well-informed persons;" and in these the Roman correspondent of the "Times" plays a notable part. For instance, that the Jesuits have a poison, the effects of which they can suspend at will, and which produces black spots all over the body; that the Pope keeps official cursers, whose occupation is to utter maledictions against his enemies; that we have chemicals and mechanism for working miracles; that we forge documents and hide them away in places where they may be found when wanted, and that in this way the catacombs, and other Catholic antiquities, can be at once explained &c., &c.

Here we have, as I have said, neither witness

nor proof of any kind; when the story is capable of disproof, that is never wanting, and its absurdity is a disproof in the remaining cases. Besides, if the rule holds good—*Judicandum est ex communiter contingentibus*—the legal presumption is that Protestant stories against Catholics are untrue. The mere fact of the periodical recurrence of these stories, always with the same features, always in time of excitement—political or controversial—against Catholics, always without proof, always disproved when sufficiently circumstantial to admit disproof, should alone persuade just and sensible men that such stories are, on the whole, unworthy of credit. That scandals occur from time to time I freely admit; but I maintain that whenever evil is done by a Catholic, it is done in spite of Catholic teaching, and is condemned by it.

The indirect proof of Dr. Littledale's accusation is drawn from our theological doctrine. He does not imply, nor for some years have I seen it suggested, that we have any other doctrine than that which is openly set forth in our writers. This was not always so. Most people, curious in ecclesiastical controversies, have heard of the *Monita Secreta* of the Jesuits, and, if they have pursued the inquiry, they will have seen that the work was a forgery of the enemies of the society. The society itself never had any other law, ordinances, or doctrines than those made known to the world either in its institute or in the published works of its theologians. I believe that every document directing or guiding its members, and the whole tenor of its spirit and practice, may be found in the library of the British Museum. It has no secret *Monita*, and even its enemies have ceased to speak about them.

Nevertheless, even in our own time, the idea was abroad that a *disciplina arcani* prevailed amongst Catholics, and, strangely enough, two very opposite views were put forward here in England regarding it. One was that the clergy had secrets which they dare not make known to the people from fear of revolt, else why the high screen round the choir, and the rites in an unknown tongue. Then came the study of architecture, and of missals, breviaries, and rituals, and as the old " view " could not be sustained, a new one had to be devised. It was now admitted that the whole doctrine found in these books was pure, noble, and scriptural, and quite in accordance with the primitive Church; but the clergy reserved this religion for themselves, and taught a lower kind of religion, full of corruptions, innovations, and in the style of St. Eligius (as traditionally explained by Protestant historians), to their ignorant hearers. It is not quite clear which of these dissolving views Dr. Littledale wishes to revive; but as he takes his stand on the ground of our public teaching, to that I will go.

We Catholics of the present day belong to the largest religious community that the world has ever seen. Others, as for instance the Buddhists, form a larger denomination, but there is no more crucial bond of unity between them than there is between the different Protestant sects. But Catholics are everywhere under the same supreme spiritual ruler, are bound by the same laws, and profess the same symbols of faith. They have their hierarchy, a living and vigilant magistracy, whose office is to guard the purity of doctrine and morals; and this, again, has its auxiliary in the assemblage of students, whose life-work is to study and teach the various ecclesiastical sciences. This last work is an object of special interest and solicitude to the rulers of the Church, for not only the purity of faith and morals, but the preservation of the traditions of the past, and the intellectual bond of union between all ages and all provinces of the Church are to a great extent sustained by it. The work of this *corpus doctum* the Church wishes to be as public and as much frequented as possible, and for this purpose, wherever it is free to do so, it opens universities, academies, and colleges, where all who wish can freely enter and listen to what is taught in the several faculties of ecclesiastical learning. The more public the teaching is, the more it is sifted, examined, and criticized, and the better is the Church pleased, if only this be done with due reverence to truth and ordinary Christian charity.

No doubt, the "secret discipline" prevailed in the early Church, and its rule had a special reference to the instruction of Catechumens, but this was due, not to the obvious propriety of instructing them step by step in the mysteries of Faith, but to the necessity of keeping those mysteries from the knowledge of the Pagans, who would use it only to blaspheme or find in it a pretext for persecution. With the conversion of the Empire this discipline wholly passed away. Henceforth the law of Christ was preached from the house-top, and it became impossible, as it was undesirable, that any portion of it or of the Church's law should be kept in the background.

The world-wide teaching of the Gospel, the organization of the community entrusted with that teaching, the methods of teaching followed by the sacred faculties, the contentions that have arisen among opposite schools of thought, and the keen and ubiquitous vigilance of the Church itself, make it simply impossible that Catholic priests can have any teaching on matters of faith, or morals, or of discipline, other than that which is openly declared in our standard works and preached in our pulpits. Again, of the thousands of converts who have joined the Church, and especially of the few who after admission have receded from it, how many have thought they were kept in the dark, or that any information regarding the "system" they thought of adopting was withheld from them at any time? I have never heard of a single instance; but I have known several such men openly express their disgust at the lies invented to deter them from becoming Catholics.

As to the charges insinuated in the two last extracts (pp. 118, 119), I need only add that our "system" has no secrets, nor can it have any. There are no "inconvenient truths" belonging to it which we care to conceal from any living being. Difficulties which may arise on the part of the Catechumen are not to be "got over" in the way suggested, but faced, and made a point of deliberate election; and "convenient misstatements" are not wanted, and even if wanted would be always sinful. Converts under instruction are not kept in the dark as to any point touching the "system" they seek to adopt, nor can they commit themselves to any obligation, act, or principle which was not fully explained to them while yet they were wholly free to accept or reject it.

The whole insinuation comes to us a mere inference from a theory shown to be baseless; it is given without a scrap of evidence or even of excusable conjecture; it originates from a discredited source, and I hold it to be the creation of the debased imagination of men who were as incapable of understanding the "Roman

System," as they style it, as were the Pagans, whose *deliria* concerning the practice of the earlier Christians Tertullian describes.

Shortly after the close of the Council of Trent there arose a new school of thought, as seems invariably to happen after each Ecumenical Council, which, under the pretext of purity of doctrine, undermined its integrity—namely, the Jansenists. Undoubtedly, the Jansenists had in their ranks men who were among the most learned, cultivated, and witty of their time. Moreover, they had on their side national vanity, and the necessity of ecclesiastical reform which neither the Pontiff nor councils could satisfy without co-operation on the part of the local clergy. From their first outset, the Jansenists found themselves pitted against the Jesuits as their most determined opponents, not certainly on the necessity of reform of manners among the clergy, but as to the right way of bringing about this reform. Yet the main point of controversy was doctrinal, and the result of it was that the Jansenists were condemned by the Church and resigned themselves to the mummy ligatures of Utrecht, and the Jesuits, thanked and honoured for their theological victory, were for a time suppressed by Clement XIV., owing to the political triumph of their opponents.

The controversy between the Jansenists and their opponents is known to ordinary Englishmen almost exclusively from the writings of Pascal and the other wits or philosophers who made common cause with him. The real matters of controversy are either wholly omitted by these sanctimonious scoffers, or kept in the background, and the subject of casuistry is brought to the front as providing ample scope for caricature and misrepresentation, and a theme for creating prejudice in many quarters. It is necessary therefore that I should say something of the doctrines of the Jansenists. They made common cause with the Gallicans in denying the spiritual authority of the Holy See all right to interfere in the national and royal customs affecting the liberties of the Church. In matters of faith, they affirmed that man was incapable of resisting the grace of God, and that all acts done apart from this irresistible grace were sinful; they exacted such conditions for justification that none but the perfect could be in the state of grace. The sacraments of penance and the Holy Eucharist were denied to the weak and infirm; but the Stoic maxim, that self-preservation overrules all law, was not forgotten, for they thought that for this end a man could dispense himself even in the Divine law.

There was another curious characteristic of these rigid moralists. When the five celebrated propositions of Jansenius were condemned by the Holy See, and his followers were obliged to abjure the heresy, they devised the theory of " obsequious silence ; " that is, they subscribed to the condemnation—on oath, I presume, as by common law required—but internally they retained belief in the teaching that their abjuration condemned and renounced. If this act of hypocrisy was confirmed by an oath, as it must generally have been, it was an undoubted perjury; in any case it was an unlawful equivocation, and a lie according to the constant teaching of Catholic theology. In any case it ill became those guilty of the act to pose as the accusers of the casuists. To speak the plain truth, the Jesuits, in defence of the legitimate authority of the Holy See, and of the merciful law of Christ that knows no acceptance of persons, had driven the Jansenists from the open field of theological controversy, and then hunted them down as they fled from one subterfuge to the other, till they were finally forced to go to Utrecht. But then came the vengeance. From one point of view the severest blow ever dealt against the Society was that given by the " Lettres Provinciales." This work did not furnish a theological or moral argument against the casuists. It was a satire of consummate cleverness and malice. No one who understands the points raised by it believes in its truth, and those who believe in it can never have taken the pains to ascertain the truth. They could see the truth at a glance by looking at any of the replies it has elicited; but this English Protestants are not likely to attempt. They have what they want in Pascal, a pretext for declaiming against casuists, and amusement too.

The doctrines of " obsequious silence," and that all things are lawful for self-preservation, are condemned by the Church, and no approved theologian holds them, or ever held them, even in favour of the Prince whom rigidists surround with such exceptional immunities; but they supply us with an excellent starting-point whereby to examine a very important matter, namely, how do Catholic priests act under extreme difficulties when the practice of truthfulness or the sacredness of an oath are at stake in their conduct? When all is said, constant practice, where life or liberty depend on the will to play fast and loose with principle, should save the martyr at least, from the imputation of insincerity. Let those who accuse Catholic priests of being untrustworthy, and bring in proof of this accusation nothing but ignorant and malicious interpretations of Catholic teaching, listen to the few facts touching this matter I have to ask their attention to. I confine myself chiefly to the story of equivocation and false swearing as illustrated in English history, for the truthfulness of English priests is that which has been directly called in question.

And I begin with an incident in the life of St. Thomas of Canterbury, not only because it comes first in the order of history, but chiefly because no event in history shows more clearly the permanent Catholic teaching on the point now under consideration. The King (Henry the Second) desired to obtain legal sanction for what he called his Royal customs, some of which were opposed to the rights and liberties of the Church and injurious to the Holy See. St. Thomas had set his face determinedly against them on these grounds. The King intimated to St. Thomas through his courtiers that the only matter that touched him was whether he should humiliate himself before the country by yielding to the Archbishop; but if the latter promised to subscribe to the customs he would not enforce them so as to inflict any injury on the Church. St. Thomas and the Bishops then agreed to sign the customs, but only with the express clause inserted in the form of subscription "Saving our order," which clause, by a legal convention, limited expressly the acceptance to such points as were compatible with the common laws of the Church. This did not satisfy the King, and he insisted on the absolute acceptance of the customs, subject only to the verbal understanding which provided that the obnoxious customs should remain a dead letter. St. Thomas in a weak moment complied, and promised "in the word of truth," a formula regarded as equivalent to an oath, to accept the customs. Henry, having obtained the promise, at once threw off the mask, and made known publicly his real purpose of assailing the rights of the Church. Upon this St. Thomas finally refused to subscribe to the customs, and in consequence was flatly accused of perjury, then murdered.

As I have already shown, amphibology cannot be used in its theological sense except to conceal a legitimate secret, and the acceptance of a legal formula must be in its plain and obvious sense, or " in the sense of the legislator expressed in the law," as the jurists say. If St. Thomas had expressed the clause " saving my order," or " saving the rights of my superior," then the required limitation would have been expressed in the oath, and all would have been right, but their omission left the oath at least ambiguous; and although, when it had been taken, it was rightly interpreted in accordance with these limitations, yet in the act of swearing, where misconception was likely to follow, the limitation should have been expressed. Catholic writers have not attempted to palliate the fault of St. Thomas, but what honest man, comparing his fall with the triumph of his murderers and accusers, will doubt as to the side on which the love of truth prevailed? *

The designs of the Tudors against the Church were radically the same as those of the Plantagenets, namely, to appropriate its revenues and subject it to the Royal control; but the Tudors went further—they destroyed the Church in the land, and introduced another fashioned by the hands of man in its place. All this demanded systematic and exterminating persecution, and throughout the whole course of the process no question of Catholic teaching came to the front so repeatedly as that of equivocation. I take one example, that of the trial of Robert Southwell, for in this matter the trials of Catholic priests were all alike, and I choose this because it is one of the oldest, best authenticated, and most illustrative of the main question. Several accounts of this trial are given by contemporary writers, but the fullest I know is that written within a year and a month of its occurrence. It is dated March 4, 1596, and is given in "Foley's Records," Series I., p. 364.

* See "Life of St. Thomas Becket," by F. Morris, Edit. 1885, c.c. xii., xiii.

Southwell was arraigned on Feb. 20, 1595, before the Lord Chief Justice Popham and the Court of Queen's Bench, for treason, the points of the arraignment being that he, being an English subject, was a priest ordained by the authority of the Pope, and was at Uxenden on a certain day. He admitted all the facts, but pleaded not guilty of treason on the ground that the law making priesthood a treason was unjust. Coke, the Attorney-General, who afterwards succeeded Popham as Chief Justice, accused Southwell of teaching the lawfulness of equivocation, which he designated as "a dangerous point of most wicked and horrible doctrine." He contended that it amounted to teaching the lawfulness of a lie or wilful perjury, that it was destructive of all government and human society, and turning to the jurors, who seem to have been London tradesmen, he warned them that by this doctrine the Papists could defraud them in buying and selling.

Southwell claimed to be allowed to explain his own teaching, and from his words, from the whole procedure in Court, and from the attitude of the Bench and the prosecution, there can be no doubt that the law of procedure as to the examination of the accused and witnesses as prescribed in the common, civil, and canon law was virtually acknowledged. Southwell quotes these laws in his justification, and on that point reduces his opponents to silence. He then points out that equivocation is not lawful unless in order to conceal a legitimate secret which the Court has no right to extort, when this is necessary to defend the rights of an innocent person, and when a refusal to answer would amount to the detection of the secret. He further observes that this doctrine supposes the theological explanation of the law of truthfulness and of an oath, and is to be limited by their determinations. The Bench and the prosecution alike, unable to answer the wisdom with which the martyr of God spoke, closed their pious ears, lest they should be defiled by such blasphemy; and Topcliffe, the brutal torture-master of the Council of Elizabeth, closed his ears also, accustomed as they were to other sounds.

The history of the judicial murders which took place in England during the time of the penal laws is no longer a sealed book, and everyone who will may satisfy himself as to the motive of equivocation on one side, and of the means taken to extort a legitimate secret on the other. It was felony to receive, harbour, or use the ministry of a priest, and the penalty of this crime was death, imprisonment, or banishment, and confiscation of all worldly goods. When a priest was captured the chief object of the Crown was to force him by dint of torture to reveal the names of all who had so dealt with him, in order that the finances of the State might be replenished. The priests, of course, submitted to any amount of torture (unless in a few cases where their minds were deranged by drugs and privation of sleep, and still fewer cases of apostasy) rather than betray the faithful to the workings of an iniquitous law; and, worn out with torture, they went to death with the street cry of " equivocator " ringing in their ears. The judges and law officers were the obsequious instruments of the Council, regularly receiving from Mr. Secretary instructions as to how they were to act, and quite ready to play each his part in the judicial murders that history lays to their charge. I might say much more as to the notorious mendaciousness, the wilful perjury, and the corruption of these men who were so shocked at the Catholic teaching on equivocation, but are not these things written in every page of the chronicles of the times?

The controversy was soon taken up outside the Law Courts, and the Anglicans had it mostly to themselves for a long time. The Catholics were hunted down and gagged, and their books destroyed. The Elizabethan tradition sped its way and prospered; and so effectually did it impress itself on the public mind, that even our language to-day shows traces of the great lie. But it was not left exclusively in the hands of controversialists. The problem as to the right of keeping a secret in certain cases had its practical, and also its philosophical, aspect, and this could not escape the attention of thinking men. Lord Bacon, who was a contemporary of Coke, examines the question from both these points of view. He lays down the necessity of keeping secrets, and says that this begets the necessity of dissimulation, "as for equivocation or oraculous speeches, they cannot hold out long. So that no man can be secret, except he give himself a little scope of dissimulation,"

&c. He ends his essay as follows: "The best composition and temperature is to have openness in fame and opinion; secresy in habit; dissimulation in reasonable use; and a power to feign if there be no remedy."*

Since the days of Bacon this has generally been the opinion of English moralists, excepting those who were engaged in controversy. In our own time, Sir Alexander Cockburn expressly defended it during the Tichborne trial, and, as I understand, with the general approval of the Bar. Men who are competent to judge see well enough that right reason must point out some means to enable a man not to betray his rights by his own words. Such betrayal nowhere enters into the convention or purpose of human intercourse by language, and the gravest interests of society are opposed to it. Theology finds the remedy in the ambiguity of language itself; English moralists go further, and, with less reverence for the provisions of Nature, allow the telling of a lie and deception.

But the accusation was kept alive in Anglican controversy where philosophy could not enter,

* "Essays, Civil and Moral," vi.

and preaching had no counterpart in practice. It was always a welcome theme with the vulgar, and a convenient opportunity for the exhibition of virtuous indignation. Several cases are within the memory of the present generation, and it may be well to recall some of them.

England will not easily forget the name of Dr. Achilli, for as long as the language lasts the portrait of that impostor, drawn by the hand of Cardinal Newman, will live to remind English Churchmen of one at least of their oracles. He came, like many others of his kind, to enlighten the people of England as to the horrors of Popery, and he had special revelations to make illustrative of the stock Anglican accusations. Equivocation served his purpose more than any other of his charges, for it was so dexterously used at his trial that none of the Catholic witnesses were believed by the jury; and if an English Protestant had not come forward to confirm a part of their evidence, Dr. Achilli would have been left free to strengthen and console the Church of England in its combat with Rome.

The question next comes to the front in the still more memorable controversy between

Canon Kingsley and Cardinal Newman. I am sorry to mention the name of Kingsley in the series of persons who have chosen to accuse Catholics of untruthfulness, for I believe he was a well-meaning, and naturally an honest man. But, following the fashion, he had flippantly committed himself to a misstatement regarding his opponent's teaching; and when this was pointed out to him he had not the moral courage to retract it, but attempted to justify it by means more censurable than his first statement. Who can forget the terrible list of "blots" proved against Canon Kingsley in his attempt to support that statement? Blots comprising equivocations, misstatements, fabrications, and, to use the words of his great opponent, exemplified as often as this question occurs, "So we come back once more to the theme of every satirist, from Juvenal to Sir Walter Scott—preaching without practising."

Dr. Kenealy renewed the controversy in his defence of the Claimant at the Tichborne trial. He hoped to discredit the evidence of priests and other Catholics by playing on the foible of English prejudice, as had been done when Dr. Achilli was forced so much against his will to prosecute Dr. Newman. But the days of Lord Campbell had passed away; another Chief Justice felt himself bound to lay down the law of common-sense, and so reverse the judgment of two at least of his predecessors, and the most unblushing imposture of our age failed to obtain countenance either from English law or public opinion, although recommended by the fascination, to the English mind, of strong denunciations of evidence given by Catholics in Courts of Justice.

But when all is said as to doctrine and teaching, the best test of truthfulness and sincerity of conviction is practice. "By their fruits you shall know them," and the fruits of virtue are acts performed in trying and crucial difficulties. It is no part of my purpose to accuse anyone, nor do I think that the Catholic cause needs that we should throw discredit on our opponents. That cause stands on its own intrinsic merits, and on these alone; but when comparison is challenged, when soul-stricken inquirers for the truth are told that Catholic priests are not to be trusted, and that they must, in spite of the promptings of their conscience, put up with misgivings and insecurity in the matter of their eternal salvation, it is time to speak plainly and give answer to the challenge. I speak of this matter with pain, but speak nevertheless I must.

How can we test most accurately the truthfulness of Catholic priests compared with that of their accusers? First of all I should say by the experience of those who have had opportunities of knowing priests well. As to Catholics themselves, distrust in their teaching is as entirely unknown as a suspicion on the part of converts whom they have received into the Church that they have been in any way kept in the dark. With us there are no " hankerers " after Anglicanism. What, for example, is the estimate which Protestant tradesmen in the neighbourhood of priests have formed of their truthfulness and honesty? However, let that pass. The Colonial Office, the officials of prisons and public hospitals, and the learned societies have frequent and excellent opportunities of judging as to the accuracy, and what may be spoken of as the "conscientious work" of different missionary bodies. They sometimes make comparisons, and these are generally of such a character as should teach caution to Anglicans when they bring charges of untruthfulness against Catholic priests. But truthfulness, like every other virtue, is best proved under severe trial; and, as it is forced upon me, I will offer to the reader a practical test by which he can judge for himself whether Catholics or their accusers value this virtue most sincerely, or set before them a higher standard of the sanctity of an oath. From the first year of Elizabeth, when the Oath of Supremacy was imposed, till the Catholic Emancipation Bill, in 1829, a long series of oaths were tendered to Catholics, some touching on matters of faith, others confining themselves to matters of mere theological opinion. As to the former, no Catholic could have taken them without knowing that he was guilty of apostasy; although in every case there was room for interpretation, quite as reasonable as, for example, that offered in the case of the Thirty-nine Articles to modern High Churchmen. For instance, Catholics might have sworn that the Sovereign was supreme head of the *Anglican Church*, without any difficulty, or that *by the law of England* no foreign prelate had spiritual jurisdiction within the realm. But Catholics knew that such restrictions were never lawful in a public declaration of religious belief, and preferred to suffer the extreme penalties of the law, death, or banishment and forfeiture of all their goods, rather than sully their conscience by having recourse to such subterfuges.

The other class of oaths is more to our point; these did not touch matters of faith, but of opinion, in which it was held to be lawful for each Catholic to hold and defend his own opinion. From the beginning to the end the crucial question under this head regarded the deposing power of the Pope. After the butchery of innocent Catholics following upon the Gunpowder Plot, James the First, with his council, seems to have honestly desired to provide some measure of toleration for his Catholic subjects. But the Royal controversialist insisted as a condition on a test oath, in which the opinion as to the deposing power was repudiated as heretical. There were two opinions current among Catholics as to the deposing power, spoken of later as the Cis-Alpine and the Trans-Alpine teaching. The former rejected absolutely the deposing power in every sense of the word; the latter acknowledged it as an indirect exercise of spiritual power, to be exercised, in exceptional cases, over Christian sovereigns, who had violated the common compact of Christendom or betrayed the spiritual rights of their subjects. Any Catholic could, with a safe conscience, have abjured the doctrine in the sense commonly ascribed to it by English Protestants, but such abjuration would be unlawful unless the exact sense in which it was made was explained by a legislative interpretation. This expedient, therefore, was not entertained. Then, again, those who rejected the dispensing power maintained that they could take the oath declaring its rejection; the others might stand aloof and bear the consequences, but they could not accuse the jurors of taking an unlawful oath. This position was so far impregnable; but those who adopted it soon discovered that although they could with a safe conscience abjure the doctrine, they could not abjure it as "heretical." In this difficulty they submitted the oath to the theological faculty of the Sorbonne and asked for a decision as to its lawfulness.

Six doctors of the University held that the oath was unlawful; forty-eight declared it to be lawful, setting forth the sense in which the word "heretical" was to be understood by the jurors. I must say for the honour of theology that the Sorbonne at this period was infected with the doctrines of Calvin and Baius, and that it was under the influence of Saint-Cyran, the master of Jansenius—the real founder of Jansenism—and the worthy father of the men who later had recourse to the subterfuge of "obsequious silence." Swearing in the sense of the juror, without a legislative interpretation, is not tolerated in theology; and it is to the honour of Catholics of all shades of opinions, that they never followed such scandalous advice. It was rejected in the present instance on the following grounds: That the clause (as to heresy) did not admit of the interpretation allotted to it by the forty-eight doctors; that it proceeded on a destination above the capacity of the vulgar, and perhaps not admitted by the magistrate who might tender the oath; and that six doctors had declared that the oath was unlawful. "Some priests," writes Cardinal Bentivoglio, many years later, "and some of the religions admitted the oath. . . . But the number of these priests is very small. . . . All the rest of the clergy have shown the greatest steadiness in opposing the oath; and the same must be said of the Regulars in general. Many of each description, contemning a thousand dangers and even death itself, have publicly confuted it," &c. ("Butler's Memoirs," Vol. I., xxviii., 1, 2, 3).

From the death of James the First till the year 1778, several overtures were made by the Ministers of State to the Catholics with a view to bring about some relaxation of the penal laws. These invariably failed, and their failure was as invariably attributed to the obstinacy of the Catholics. It is quite certain that, so far as the contemplated measures of relief extended, the only difficulty lay in the abjuration of the deposing power of the Pope, and that this was the only point of disagreement among Catholics themselves. Charles Butler, relating the unfortunate result of these conferences, says, mournfully, that they were due to disagreements among the Catholics themselves, and to the arrogance or narrowness of some. This most trustworthy historian and upright Catholic was an advanced Cis-alpine, who thoroughly rejected the opinion in favour of the deposing power, and would naturally designate as narrowness the objections of many Catholics to abjure it as fully as he was prepared to do. He would also regard as arrogance the peremptory refusal of the Vicars Apostolic, who mostly favoured the Cis-alpine opinions, to refuse their sanction to an oath, which, whatever their own opinions might be, many of the faithful committed to their charge could not conscientiously take.

But in the year 1778 a comprehensive measure of relief for Catholics became law, and an oath was proposed, which, so far as the abjured teaching was concerned, no Catholic need object to. The clause touching this matter was as follows: "I further declare that it is no article of my faith, and that I do renounce, reject, and abjure the opinion that princes excommunicated by the Pope and Council, or any other authority of the See of Rome, or by any authority whatsoever, may be deposed, or murdered by their subjects or any person whatsoever; and I do declare that I do not believe that the Pope of Rome, or any other foreign prince, prelate, state or potentate, hath, or ought to have, any temporal or civil jurisdiction, power, superiority or pre-eminence, directly or indirectly, within this realm."

The obvious tenor of this oath was materially different in several respects from that rejected by the Catholics under James the First. The theory regarding the deposing power as held by the Trans-alpine Catholic is not repudiated, still less abjured as a heresy. The abjuration exacted regarded imputed consequences of excommunication which all Catholics rejected, and the second part of the clause was confined to the temporal and civil jurisdiction of the Pope in these realms. His spiritual authority, whether direct or indirect, remained unchallenged.

In the year 1821, a Bill was introduced into Parliament with the object of opening to Catholics the higher preferments in the public service, and it was proposed to effect this by passing for them a special oath of allegiance suited to their religious convictions. Conferences were held between the Parliamentary promoters of this measure and the Catholic committee, and the only difficulty felt on either side regarded the terms in which the abjuration of the deposing power was to be expressed. The first draft of the oath furnished to the

Catholic committee contained an unqualified denial of the spiritual jurisdiction of the Pope; and to this, of course, they could not assent. It was then represented to them that the clause regarding the spiritual authority was to be interpreted by an "injunction" or "explanation" of Queen Elizabeth respecting the oath of allegiance, published in the first year of her reign (1559), by which the abjuration was limited to matters touching the independence and security of the Sovereign.

The Catholics would not accept an oath apparently opposed to their belief, and resting for its interpretation in their sense on an act, in itself of doubtful sincerity, of which the Catholics in the reign of Elizabeth made no account, and which now rested on the verbal declaration of the promoters of the Bill, and on the authority of the law officers of the Crown. They, therefore, asked that an express "legislative interpretation" might be inserted in the Bill, setting forth the restricted sense in which the denial of the spiritual power of the Pope was to be understood. This was acceded to by a resolution of the Committee of the House of Commons on the second of March. The "legislative interpretation," however, thus provided remained ambiguous; it rested on the injunction of Elizabeth, and this the Catholics could not accept as sincere; in one place this injunction seemed to deny the abjuration of the rightful authority of the Pope, but presently it claimed for the Sovereign the spiritual jurisdiction claimed by Henry VIII. and Edward VI. This objection was also admitted, and the "legislative interpretation" which the Catholics called for was inserted in the form of the oath as follows: "And I do declare that no foreign power, &c., hath or ought to have any jurisdiction, &c., ecclesiastical or spiritual, within this realm, that in any manner or for any purpose conflicts or interferes with the duty of full and undivided allegiance which by the laws of the realm is due to his Majesty, &c."

The Bill passed through the three readings of the House of Commons, but was thrown out by the Lords, and so lost; yet the history of its passage through the Lower House throws a singular light on the estimate Catholics have of an oath, and of their uncompromising adherence, under the gravest difficulties, to the theological principles ruling its lawful use.

I will add one more example, taken from modern French history, in illustration of the estimate of an oath held by Catholic priests. In August, of year 1790, "the Civil Constitution of the Clergy" became law in France. The avowed tenor of this enactment—as its title indicated, and as its supporters formally announced—was in no way to invade the spiritual domain of the Church, but only to provide for the better civil organization of the clergy. It contained no provision that was not, according to the Gallican school of theology, in harmony with the practice of the primitive Church. It did not meddle with matters of faith or morals, or sacred rites, or the constitution of the hierarchy. It contained the saving clause, "all without prejudice to the unity of Faith, and to the communion that should exist with the visible head of the universal Church [the Roman Pontiff], as shall appear hereinafter" (T. 1., a. iv.). All beneficiaries were to make to the Bishops profession of "the Catholic Apostolic and Roman Faith," which meant, according to the canon law then in force, the profession of Pius IV.

The gravamen of this constitution was that

the national Legislature, notwithstanding its disavowal of interfering in spiritual matters, claimed to originate a new circumscription of the dioceses and of minor benefices, suppressing some, creating others anew, alienating Church property, and forbidding bishops to obtain canonical institution by Papal authority. In this, even according to Gallican opinions, there was a gross invasion of the spiritual domain by the civil powers, and as at this time the mass of the French clergy had renounced the older Gallican opinions, the graver difficulty occurred to them, namely, how the new bishops could obtain spiritual jurisdiction without Papal institution? Yet these difficulties could be got over. It was felt that, under the circumstances, the Holy See would not withhold jurisdiction from the bishops on the mere ground of defect in their canonical institution, and for the rest the clergy could passively submit to the ordinances of the civil constitution, as men will sometimes submit to be despoiled rather than to contend.

But another difficulty arose: the following oath, to be taken by all beneficiaries, under penalty of forfeiture and privation of office, was appended to the constitution:—"I swear to watch with care over the faithful confided to my direction. I swear to be faithful to the nation, to the law, and to the king. I swear to maintain to the best of my power the French constitution, and expressly the decrees regarding the civil constitution of the clergy." This oath the great mass of the clergy flatly refused to take, and in place of it proposed their own form known as "the restricted oath." It ran—"I swear to watch with care over the faithful confided to my direction *by the Church;* to be faithful to the nation, the law, and the king, and to maintain to the best of my power, *in all that concerns the political order,* the constitution decreed by the National Assembly and accepted by the King, *excepting expressly matters essentially dependent on the spiritual authority.*"

This form makes no change in the original oath except by the expression of the restrictions which I have italicised, all which, as was stated in the National Assembly, were virtually contained in the earlier form. The difference between the two forms may appear very trifling, but it did not appear so to the priests of France. They could not act upon any unlegalized interpretation as to the meaning of their oath, nor swear in any sense but that expressly signified in the law. The form proposed by the clergy was rejected by the Assembly, and the first oath " pure and simple," was enacted. The result was that more than fifty thousand of the French clergy were stripped of their revenues, deprived of office, and forced into banishment. " We have their goods," said Mirabeau, " but they have kept their honour." Honour they certainly deserved, but I believe it was little in their thoughts when they made the great choice. The love of honour cannot explain the act of men giving up home, comfort, and country, to wander among strange people as beggars and outcasts. Still less could honour induce fifty thousand devoted and laborious priests to relinquish the flocks confided to them, and leave Christianity in France at the mercy of hirelings or atheists. Their true motive was this—they would not sully their conscience by taking a sacrilegious oath, that is, a legally tendered oath taken with restrictions or interpretations not fully and expressly warranted by the law itself. (Jager, " Histoire de l'Église de France pendant la Révolution," A.D. 1790, 1791.)

This series of struggles for conscience' sake brings out, if I don't greatly mistake, the law by which Catholic priests are guided, and to which they have, as a body, been faithful from the Council of Antioch to our own days, under the severest trials that man can be subjected to; a law clearly defined by theologians and canonists, not only as affecting professions of faith or articles of religion, but comprehending every legally-tendered oath, whether the law enforcing or allowing it be just or unjust. This law of swearing means not only that we speak the truth, and nothing but the truth, that we are pledged to tell, but also that we are to guard ourselves against being misunderstood by the ignorant or misrepresented by the malicious; and that if there is any divergence between the interior conception of the mind and the spoken word, that divergence must be expressly reconciled either by the letter of the law or the form of the oath, or else by a publicly acknowledged legal convention.

I have tried to put beyond all doubt the law as well as the practice of Catholic priests, so far as it concerns the virtue of truthfulness in simple speech and oath. I have not touched on the yet higher function of the same virtue, the preservation in the heart in its purity and integrity "of every word that cometh from the mouth of God," for this function of truthfulness does not come directly within my purpose. But I have been goaded to say what I have said by the cruel and cowardly slander uttered by men like Dr. Littledale against us. And now, having said so much, I have every right to ask what is the theory and the practice of our accusers in similar difficulties, or in cases most nearly approaching them?

I feel that I cannot well approach this subject without seeming to include Anglican clergymen in general in the countercharge; yet this is not my purpose, nor do I feel that I have a right to adopt such a course. Dr. Littledale, and many like him, assume that we have a standard of truthfulness far inferior to their own. The dishonesty I wish to put my finger upon lies chiefly in this assumption. The majority of the Anglican clergy do not, I believe, approve of Dr. Littledale's proceedings, and even feel that they are compromised by them. I have no more right to arraign such men before the tribunals of canon or Roman law than they have to judge

St. Alphonsus by English law. Let each side stand or fall by its own standard; but to compare one standard of truthfulness with another, or to estimate fairly the standard of any body of men by their uniform practice, surely can in no sense be regarded as recrimination. I will therefore ask attention, as the nearest parallel I can find in the Anglican Church to the oaths of which I have so far been speaking, to the subscription to the Thirty-nine Articles signed, I believe, by all Anglican clergymen.

It is only right to acknowledge that many Anglicans deny these articles to be articles of faith, or to constitute a profession of faith, but only, as Bishop Forbes affirms them to be, "articles of religion." Again, it is affirmed that some of them are mere conclusions or statements of no religious authority. Certainly, the law imposing the articles is unjust, and therefore, according to our rule, no real law. Lastly, I understand that the subscription to the articles does not imply an oath, but only a solemn declaration of assent, and it may be that the declaration contains a clause explaining away the very emphatic language of the royal edict by which the articles became the law of the Anglican Church. Giving all due weight to these considerations, the facts remain that subscription to the articles means a solemn declaration made to one acknowledged to be an ecclesiastical superior and a legally constituted public official. It is a voluntary statement, not made under compulsion, not necessary to preserve natural or acquired rights, but only as an opening to church preferment and ecclesiastical livings, or other remunerative offices in the Anglican Church. No one is compelled to make it, and if he declines to do so, the ordinary career of an Englishman and promotion in the public service is open to him without prejudice. The subscription then is, in the fullest sense of the words, free and deliberate.

So far, no one, I take it, will call my statements as to the thirty-nine articles in question; and I feel on equally safe ground in adding that they are accepted by a very large number of candidates for orders who absolutely disbelieve, reject, and detest some of the teaching contained in them in its obvious and literal sense. Here we have, I do not say an undeniable fact, but the statement of the fact by the subscribers themselves; and the open acknowledgment of the divergence between their convictions and the *wording* of the article deserves to be recorded to their credit. But still the procedure exhibits a standard of truthfulness which is not our standard, the reconciliation of both being to us often a matter of bewilderment.

So far as I can understand the High Church standpoint on this problem, it is as follows:— The articles, they say, are a compromise between the tenets of the Catholic and Puritan parties in the Anglican Church; they are articles of peace intended to mark the comprehensiveness and not the exclusiveness of their Church. They are capable, therefore, of a twofold interpretation suited to the views of each party, and each party can subscribe to them in his own sense.

This is so far clear; but to express it in theological language it should be said that the articles are amphibologies, and that in giving assent to them the use of equivocation is recommended. This I say, although couched in other language, is the unquestionable and avowed position assumed by the High Church clergymen. I do not suppose my statement as to the position assumed will be ever questioned.

The controversy as to the interpretation of the articles, the claims of the High Church to interpret them in their own sense, and the sense they put upon them, are well known. Bishop Forbes, in the epistle dedicatory of his explanation of the articles, addressed to Dr. Pusey, lays down the canon of interpretation. "They must be read," he says, " with the gloss of antecedent faith and preconceived notion. Just as in our own time men have read them with the preconceived notion of the low-church school, and so have imported into them meanings which their letter will not bear ; so at the time of their enforcement they must have been read with the deep consciousness of the old traditional Christianity, which had obtained in England since the days of St. Augustine of Canterbury," &c. (p. 21).

This opens to our view a spacious field for interpreting a solemn profession of religious adhesion. It is difficult to see where anyone need stop, or in what sense adhesion to the articles is in any way a test of assent. We have only to put ourselves in the position of Laud or Parker, or, if we prefer it, in the position of John Knox, nay, of St. Augustine, of

Lanfranc, or of St. Anselm, and why not of Pope Gregory, who sent Augustine to England, and holding the belief of any one of them we can subscribe to the articles in "meanings that the letter will not bear."

I do not, of course, question the right of any body of men to interpret their own formulas of belief and to hold them in whatever sense they choose, but a public test tendered by legal authority admits, according to our standard, of no interpretation but that expressly given it by the law. I claim a right to explain my own formula, but if the formula of another comes to me as a legal test, and I accept it, I am bound to do so in his sense or else to refuse to altogether. The fathers of the Council of Rimini accepted in good faith a formula fraudulently designed to entrap them. They never suspected its ambiguity or they would have died rather than sign it, but when its latent meaning was made known to them they considered themselves tainted with the external note of heresy until they had formally revoked their act. Pope Liberius has been accused—whether rightly or not is not to my present purpose—of signing an amphibologous judgment in order to regain his liberty. Those who believed the story, as probably St. Hilary, pronounced him in consequence to be fallen from his high office and to have incurred *anathema*. I have already spoken of the fall and penance of St. Thomas of Canterbury. Bishop Forbes tells us that Sancta Clara, an able Catholic theologian, asserts that the Thirty-nine Articles, "by the exercise of allowable casuistry, are compatible with Tridentine doctrine" (*Ibid.*, p. 7). I cannot deny the Bishop's statement, though I have been unable to find the assertion in Sancta Clara, but I am sure that the Catholic schools of theology would unanimously reject his opinions. So far as I can ascertain Sancta Clara's position, it was this, that in view of corporate reunion, if a public and authoritative declaration were made of the Catholic sense of the articles, subscription to them on the part of Anglicans would constitute no bar to reconciliation. In this opinion too he was certainly mistaken, yet it is something that he saw the necessity of a legal interpretation to justify the attribution of a Catholic meaning to the articles.

There is no more sacred trust confided to the

Church than to preserve in its integrity the deposit of faith committed to its keeping, and this means not only its witnessing to the world each particular truth of that deposit, but also its securing that each one admitted to its communion partakes in its integrity in the common faith. In this matter it never has tolerated, and never will tolerate, any ambiguity, nor allow one of its members to subscribe to a formula that may with any show of reason be taken in an erroneous sense. Where ground for suspicion as to matters of faith force themselves on its attention the Church is accustomed to exact abjuration, and in the test proposed the *stylus* of its law declares the illegality of all interpretation on the part of jurors or others not having legislative or judicial authority.

In the declaration of Charles the First enforcing subscription to the articles on the clergy of the establishment this *stylus* is imitated, and the cause of its adoption throws a curious light on the law regulating this interpretation. James the First had sent deputies to the Synod of Dort, where questions regarding predestination were violently agitated. On their return to England the controversy was carried on with much vehemence within the Anglican communion, each party claiming the authority of the Thirty-nine Articles on its side. We learn from Bishop Burnet that the object of the declaration and the enforcement of the articles was to put an end to this controversy, or, as we should say of a Pontifical decree in a parallel case among ourselves, to impose silence on both sides (Burnet, Introduction to "Exposition of the Articles").

The King states in the declaration that notwithstanding the differences that had been raised "all clergymen within our realm have always most willingly subscribed to the articles established, which is an argument to us, that they all agree in the true, usual, literal meaning of the said articles, and that even in those curious points in which the present differences lie, men of all sorts take the articles of the Church of England to be for them, which is an argument again that none of them intend any desertion of the articles established." Wherefore, to put an end to such disputes, His Majesty orders "that no man hereafter shall either print or preach to draw the article aside anyway, but shall submit to it in the plain and full meaning thereof, and shall not put his own sense or comment to be the meaning of the article, but shall take it in the literal and grammatical sense."

This declaration is the law under which the articles are subscribed to, and it fully justifies us drawing the following conclusions. First, the articles in question express in their true, usual, literal sense, the religious belief of the Anglican clergy from the date of their formation in the year 1562 till their promulgation by Charles I. in 1628; that at the latter date the King had every reason to believe that the clergy would willingly subscribe to them in the same sense. That so far from the law providing an express interpretation to enable dissenters from the plain and literal sense to subscribe to them, the law peremptorily forbids any such interpretation or drawing aside of the article to any sense but that declared.

The prohibition of the law is about as express as any legal prohibition can be, and its direct and deliberate violation is equally unquestionable. The advice of Bishop Forbes is to read the articles "with a gloss," the gloss being dependent not on the plain meaning of the article, but on "antecedent faith and preconceived notion," and which imports into the articles "meanings which their letter will not bear." I have no need to draw out the antagonism between the law of the English Church and the practice of Anglican clergymen who pledge themselves to obey it; neither have I a right to arraign Anglicans before the bar of theology, or canon, or, much less, civil law, for they disavow the competence of all such tribunals, in religious matters. But I have to deal with the notion of a solemn test tendered and accepted in the name of some law, and I must say that the law of Nature—that is right reason—and the *jus gentium* condemn such declaration as that of which I have been speaking as wrong, and should its unlawfulness fade from the consciences of men, then I say let religious tests be discontinued as useless, nay, as a very mockery of the truthfulness of God.

I will take one example among many of the extravagance to which this forbidden system of glossing and interpreting is extended. Article XXXI. enjoins assent to the following proposition—" Wherefore the sacrifices of masses in which it was commonly said that the priest did offer Christ for the quick and the dead to have remission of pain or guilt were blasphemous fables and dangerous deceits." It is well to notice that the literal translation of the latin text of the article is—"blasphemous figments and pernicious impostures."

The Catholic teaching on the Sacrifice of the Mass is set forth in a series of decrees and canons in the twenty-second session of the Council of Trent, held in the year 1562, the year in which the Thirty-nine Articles were approved by the Anglican Church. The doctrine of the Council is that the mass is a sacrifice in which the priest offers up Christ as a propitiatory and satisfactory sacrifice for the quick and the dead, and it pronounces anathema against those who speak of it as a "blasphemy" or "imposture." In the Profession of Faith published by Pius IV. in 1564 we have the doctrine of the Council summarized in the following article: "I equally profess that in the sacrifice of the mass there is offered to God a true, proper, and propitiatory sacrifice for the quick and the dead."

Each article, that of Trent and the Anglican Church, was the outcome of prolonged and notorious controversy. It was a question among all others of central and conspicuous importance, for on it depended the true notion of the priesthood, the episcopacy, and of the hieratic character of the Church. Never in the history of controversy, not even at Nicæa, Ephesus, or Chalcedon, were two counter propositions more diametrically opposed or vigorously defended or attacked in their plain and literal sense. What each proposition meant in the mouths of its supporters no man in Christendom has ever sincerely doubted.

Now, if anyone will read the explanation of Article XXXI. by Bishop Forbes he will find that according to him a man may hold the entire doctrine of the Council of Trent, and nevertheless subscribe with a safe conscience to the Article. He thinks it quite sufficient to point out by "antecedent faith and preconceived notion" what the Catholic truth is, and having shown it gives us to understand that the Article which denounces it as a fraud and an imposture may be lawfully subscribed to.

I have already disclaimed any intention, for I have no right, to pronounce judgment on Anglican clergymen in their own affairs. I know well that many among them heartily disapprove of Dr. Littledale's ill-advised publications, and that they sympathize with us Catholic priests in the unmerited attacks we are subjected to from their own co-religionists. But I cannot forget that they all—for all of them, I suppose, have subscribed to the Articles—have borne witness that we, in the most sacred and venerable act of sacrifice, perpetuate a fable and an imposture, while many of them go as far as they can in doing what they condemn in us, and denounce in the words quoted. It would be interesting at least to know whether Dr. Littledale, the accuser of others, agrees with the Article in its literal and grammatical sense, or else with Bishop Forbes' explanation of it. I will end by quoting an old canon taken from the writings of St. Gregory the Great, who sent St. Augustine to England, and which applies no less to solemn declarations than to oaths: "No matter with what craftiness of words a man may take an oath, God who is the witness of the conscience receives the statement in the same sense as he to whom the oath is made" ("Decretum Gratiani," 11, 22, 95, c. 9).

POSTSCRIPT.

Since this essay went to the press the case of Father Keller has occurred, and has met with much and varied criticism in the newspapers; and as it touches in several points the matters I have been trying to explain, I trust the reader, who has accompanied me so far, will not be unwilling to have placed before him the theological *criteria* by which it should be estimated.

I take, as the starting point of the whole inquiry, the position assumed by Father Keller in the witness-box of the Dublin Bankruptcy Court, as reported in the "Times" of March 21st. On a certain question being proposed, Father Keller refused to answer, "because it might drift him into answers which would disclose secrets which in honour he could not disclose, or declare with honour to his sacred profession." Later on he explained that his answer might tend to elicit from him matters which came to his knowledge "simply and solely because I am a priest." There was no reference to the seal of sacramental confession; no reliance on the well-known fact that the witness was a parish priest. He took his stand on the fact that professional secrets had been confided to him as a priest (holding public office in the Church), and he declared in the solemn language of an oath that his conscience forbade him to divulge such secrets. Here, then, is the unequivocal standpoint of the witness, and I shall now try to explain the theological and legal ground on which he rests.

The general question, theologically considered, is, how far is a professional man bound to conceal secrets known as "secrets of counsel," and by what law is he so bound? These are secrets confided in order to obtain professional advice for the guidance of the inquirer. It may be that a person consults a lawyer, and in doing so discloses facts which, if known to a Court, would prejudice his cause; or he may make known to a medical man a secret disease contracted by some shameful excess; or he may seek the advice of a clergyman in some moral or spiritual perplexity. In all these cases I assume that counsel is sought for from one publicly constituted in office, and by his profession qualified to give such counsel, and that the inquirer leaves in possession of his adviser a secret which cannot be made known without grave injury to the former.

It stands to reason that in the cases supposed the adviser is bound under a grave obligation to preserve the secret; but on what grounds? The grounds are—the nature and the circumstances of the interview, the relations of the persons, and the implied contract between them. These three grounds of the obligation make it clear that it springs from the law of nature, and binds independently of any human or positive law. They also indicate that the law is not absolute, and therefore forbidding the revelation of the secret as intrinsically wrong, but that it is a general law admitting of exceptions, where there is a just cause for making the secret known. Theologians and Jurists commonly admit two exceptions, and two only, namely, where the revelation of the secret is necessary to avert serious injury, (1) private or (2) public.

All positive law, though in various degrees, recognizes the privilege of secrets of counsel so far as to release sworn witnesses from all obligation to divulge them. The canon and common civil law are, as usual, in perfect harmony in this respect. By the canon law, except in the two cases just mentioned, no Ecclesiastical Superior, under the title of oath or vow, or any other claim, can oblige a priest to divulge a secret of counsel. The Roman law prescribes the same in the case of witnesses amenable to its tribunals.

The reason of this lenity, as explained by the Jurists, is, that in addition to the reasons alleged in proof of the natural law, it is much better for human society, and, in the main, more conducive to the ends of justice, that men in their difficulties should, without any fear of defamation, have recourse to approved and experienced professional men as advisers, rather than abstain from such counsel through fear of denunciation.

The English law is less lenient in this matter than any other law I know of. It recognizes the privilege of professional confidence, entrusted to the legal profession, but to no other. The first case, then, that I propose to consider is whether the English law and the ruling of the Judge in an English Court of Justice is a "just cause" for a medical man to reveal as a witness a secret of counsel? I have here, in the concrete case, no authority to guide me, but only the general principles that I have already laid down. I think it a public calamity and a scandal that medical men should be forced to give such evidence as they sometimes have to give, for example, in the Divorce Court. This is not the purpose of their profession nor to its honour, and it is of little service to the ends of justice. But we must take the law as it stands. We must remember that medical men constantly give this kind of evidence freely and without protest; and above all we must remember that in the discharge of their professional duties they act under license from the State, and are responsible to it for the proper discharge of those duties. In view of these facts I cannot say that the action of medical men in the case supposed is condemned by sound ethics, nor can I see any other course open to them. It is, however, to be hoped that before long some of our legislators will take to heart the honour of the medical profession and remove this scandal from our legal code.

Coming next to the case of a Catholic priest in England, ordered by a Judge to reveal in Court a secret of counsel, it will appear at first sight that his case stands on a very different footing from that of a medical witness. There can be, I suppose, no doubt that before the Reformation the law respected the professional secrets of priests, and that the change introduced into the law at the Reformation was *in odium sacerdotii*, and if this was the sole motive it would, therefore, be regarded by Catholics as unjust and no law.

Nevertheless, to take our stand purely on the civil law, subsequent acquiescence or established custom might have convalidated a law originally unjust. Has any such acquiescence or custom prevailed? Unquestionably not. Not only in England since the Reformation, but at all times and under every system of law, Catholic priests have, as a rule, with the two exceptions already given, refused to declare secrets of confidence entrusted to them. The original injustice, therefore, of the present English law has never been removed by the introduction of any legitimate custom.

In the next place, Catholic priests, in their strictly professional duties, are not subject to any civil authority, except so far as these duties involve civil consequences. They do not assume their professional duties in virtue of any civil license. The civil law acknowledges that in matters purely professional they are amenable to their own tribunals exclusively; and should, in the discharge of those duties strictly professional, a collision be inevitable between the canon law and the law of the land, they are bound in conscience to obey the former. The observance on the part of a priest of a secret of counsel (excepting the cases already mentioned) is of this character; and even where the law of the land is not tainted by original injustice its mandate is not a just cause for revealing a secret such as I suppose privileged by the law of nature and of the Church.

In Ireland the case stands on a different footing. It is now fully acknowledged, and seems to have been admitted on all sides in the late proceedings in the Dublin Bankruptcy Court, that by the common practice secrets of counsel confided to priests are privileged in the Courts of Justice. In Ireland, therefore, even the civil law exempts a priest from answering questions involving the disclosure of such secrets. The point at issue between Father Keller and the Court was not as to the existence of the privilege, but as to whether the question he refused to answer was or was not covered by it.

I now leave the general question, to come to the particular facts which led to Father Keller's imprisonment. His appearance in the witness-box was ostensibly in discharge of a civil duty; in reality the duty he discharged was primarily and directly ecclesiastical. As to the manner in which he acquitted himself, his ecclesiastical superiors have in the most public way expressed their unqualified approval. This, I think, should make Catholics, if no others, cautious as to adverse criticisms on his conduct, or at least have deterred Catholics, apparently quite ignorant of the canon law, from quoting it misadvisedly in his condemnation, and this in the public newspapers, Catholic and Protestant. For my own part, I should not have ventured to speak of this case but for the comments, scandalous or absurd, which have appeared upon it, and which seem to have made it, to a certain extent, public property. But for this, I should have shrunk from the thought of expressing in public any opinion upon it, and in any case I deny the right of individual Catholics to ignore or call in question the judgments of ecclesiastical superiors in ecclesiastical matters, or submit them to the very unstable tribunal of public opinion.

Following the order of events, the first charge against Father Keller is that he refused to obey the summons of the Court to appear as witness, and only appeared when compelled to do so. I cannot say that he was bound to adopt this course, but I maintain that it was a wise and proper course, foreseeing as he did the purpose of the citation. He expected to be sworn to declare that which his conscience told him he should not declare, and though he had his remedy in inserting an express restriction in the oath, he was right in taking his stand at the first stage of the procedure, and avoiding, unless under compulsion, direct collision with the judicial authority.

He is next accused of having insisted on an express restriction as to the obligation of his oath. In doing so he acted according to the invariable practice of Christians placed in a like difficulty. St. Thomas of Canterbury, as I have urged on p. 136, failed in his duty because in his oath he omitted the restriction: "Saving the honour of my order;" and for this omission he condemned himself, and is blamed by Catholic historians. Father Keller insisted on the clause, and would not swear without expressing it; and yet even Catholics are found who dare to condemn him.

Lastly, the question which Father Keller refused to answer was in itself no matter of confidence; the answer to it could disclose no professional secret, yet he refused to answer it, because his answer, if given, would drift him into a forbidden disclosure. Had he answered this question, another of the same tenor might follow, and then a third and a fourth, all outside any direct revelation of the secret of counsel which he was bound to keep; nevertheless, a lawyer having the four answers in evidence might furnish the Court with a convincing proof of the fact revealed under the secret of counsel. Is it lawful for one bound to keep his neighbour's secret to betray it piecemeal in this fashion? A Catholic lawyer, writing in the "Tablet" tells us that it is not only lawful, but a duty to do so, and quotes the canon law in support of this opinion. I have unbounded confidence in the justice of the canon law and in scientific casuistry, but if I thought that a single text, or a single approved writer, supported this grossly immoral conclusion, my confidence would be broken, and I should keep silence on these matters for the rest of my life.

So far as I can understand the point at issue between Father Keller and the Court, it was this: Father Keller refused to answer a question for the reason stated, and the Court disallowed his objection on the ground that the question was not comprehended in the privilege of a secret of counsel, confided to the witness in his priestly character. I cannot see that the objection of the Judge was unreasonable or unduly harsh. I believe that in an Ecclesiastical Court the Judge might, in a contentious cause, rule in the same sense. It may be well, then, to consider what would be the duty of a witness—let us suppose a priest—if the ruling of an Ecclesiastical Judge were opposed to the ruling of the Court of Conscience? The collision sometimes happens, because the evidence attainable in the external Court is less complete, and therefore the Judge is thrown upon presumptions, which sometimes fail to reach the truth, and which have no place in the Court of Conscience. When such collision occurs a Christian is bound to abide by the dictate of conscience, and not to obey the ruling of the Canonical Court, even though he should be sentenced to do so under the severest ecclesiastical censures. These he may regard as merely penal inflictions; and he must obey his conscience, no matter what evil consequences may follow. The case is considered by canonists of one who is told by his confessor to disobey the precept of an Ecclesiastical Judge prescribing a certain course to be followed under penalty of excommunication, and they lay down that the subject in such conflict of the different Courts is bound to follow the ruling of the Court of Conscience.

It cannot, therefore, be a matter of surprise that collision will sometimes occur between the Civil Courts and the Court of Conscience; and to return to the case in point, when we remember that no Ecclesiastical Judge can bind a priest to reveal a secret of counsel, and that no Civil Court has authority over a priest in matters strictly belonging to his ecclesiastical duties, and, lastly, that the witness alone can safely judge as to what answer might lead to the detection of the secret, it will be clear that the point must finally be left to the conscience of the witness, and that he must abide by the dictates of his conscience. There is no question here of the conscience of a fanatic or of an ignorant person. There is no longer any question as to a rule of conscience; the question is whether a witness, who alone knows the truth, is to be believed when he swears that such a question leads to the violation of a secret? When there is a strong presumption against the witness the Court has its own remedy. If this case were in the Canonical Courts all the legal presumptions would be on the side of the witness. Why they seem to be different in English law I cannot comprehend.

This essay was indirectly occasioned by the fact that a respected priest in London received in his official reception-room a visit from a lady, who asked to be instructed and received into the Catholic Church. Much indignation was excited because he complied with this request without informing the lady's husband. My work ends with the unforeseen reference to Father Keller's case. Should I ever find myself in the position of either of these men, I trust I shall have the courage to follow their example.

END.

THE CATHOLIC STANDARD LIBRARY.

UNDER the above title it is proposed to issue a series of Catholic Standard Works, consisting of Foreign Translations, Standard Reprints, and Original Works.

It is intended to publish 3 vols. yearly, in demy 8vo, of from 450 to 500 pp.

The price to Subscribers will be 25s. yearly for 3 vols.; to Non-subscribers, 12s. each vol.

The works will be printed in the best style of the typographic art, on paper made for the purpose, and bound in cloth, Roxburgh style.

The first year's issue will be

A Universal Church History,

By the Abbé ROHRBACHER, Doctor of Theology of the University of Louvain, &c., &c. Translated by various hands, and edited by ALBANY J. CHRISTIE, S.J., M.A., Oxon, sometime Fellow of Oriel College.

Although there have been many editions of Rohrbacher's great work in the original French, as well as German and Italian translations, it has not hitherto been done into English, and it has been well said that such an edition will be a great gain to English literature.

VOLS. I. & II.—FROM THE CREATION OF THE WORLD TO THE TIMES OF THE PROPHET JEREMIAH.

In the Press.

A Commentary on the Holy Gospels,

By JOHN MALDONATUS, S.J., Translated and Edited from the original Latin by GEORGE J. DAVIE, M.A., Exeter College, Oxford, one of the Translators of the Library of the Fathers.

VOL. I. *In the Press.*

John Maldonatus was a learned Spanish Jesuit, born in 1534, died in 1583. He taught Philosophy in Paris to crowds of listeners. He was called to Rome by Pope Gregory XIII. to superintend the Publication of the Septuagint. His works were published posthumously. Among all the commentators few have so happily explained the general sense of the four Gospels; he allows no difficulty to pass without examining it thoroughly.

From the marked success given to the publication of the translation of Cornelius à Lapide's Commentary on the Gospels, the projectors believe a hearty welcome will be given to these new translations by English readers and students.

JOHN HODGES, 25, Henrietta Street, Covent Garden, W.

A Welcome Present to the Clergy, Religious Communities, Newly-Ordained Priests, Deacons, and Theological Students.

A TRANSLATION INTO ENGLISH OF THE

Great Commentary upon the Holy Scriptures
of Cornelius à Lapide. By the Rev. T. W. MOSSMAN, B.A., Oxon.

Vol. I., II., III. Demy 8vo, each 12s., completing SS. Matthew and Mark's Gospels.

St. John's Gospel and Three Epistles. Two Vols., 24s.

St. Luke's Gospel. One Vol., 12s. Completing the Gospels. (*Just ready.*)

"Really the Editor has succeeded in presenting the public with a charming book. When we open his pages we find ourselves listening to voices from all ages of the Church's history, from the pulpits where St. Athanasius and St. Augustin defended the faith against its earliest traducers, from the lecture halls where St. Thomas and Suarez cast the self-same doctrine into the most rigid scientific form, from the cloister where St. Bernard sweetly nourished the devotion of his monks, and we see how they derive their inspiration from the same Divine source, the Holy Scriptures. We have been accustomed to regard à Lapide for consultation rather than to be read. But in the compressed form, clear and easy style, and excellent type in which it now appears, it is a book we can sit down and enjoy."—*The Month.*

A Chronicle of the English Benedictine Monks,
from the renewing of their Congregation in the Days of Queen Mary to the Death of James II.; being the Chronological Notes of DOM. BENNETT WELDON, O.S.B., a Monk of Paris. Edited, from a Manuscript in the Library of St. Gregory's Priory, Downside, by a MONK of the same Congregation. Demy 4to, handsomely printed. Second Edition, 12s. *Now ready.*

The Helliotropium, or Conformity, of the Human Will to the Divine. By JEREMY DREXELIUS. Translated from the Original Latin by R. N. SHUTE, B.A. With a Preface by the late Bishop FORBES. Second and Cheaper Edition, crown 8vo, 7s. 6d.

The Autobiography of an Alms-Bag; or, Sketches of Church and Social Life in a Watering-Place. By the Author of " Recreations of the People," &c. Crown 8vo, 3s. 6d.

"A clever book. Sketchy anecdotic, chatty, humorous, and suggestive. We read of many topics, nearly all full of interest."—*Literary World.*

"Overflows with good stories effectively told, and most of them brought into good and useful purpose."—*Guardian.*

Notes on Ingersoll. By the Rev. L. A. LAMBERT, of Waterloo, New York. Revised and Reprinted from the 50th Thousand American Edition. Second Edition. Price 1s. 6d.; or in limp cloth, 1s.

"Every possible objection brought by Ingersoll against Christianity is completely crushed by Lambert."—*Guardian.*

Vol. IV., demy 8vo, 552 pp., 15s., completing the Work, now ready.

Historical Portraits of the Tudor Dynasty and the Reformation Period. By S. HUBERT BURKE. Complete in Four Vols., price £2 17s. Either volume sold separately. "Time unveils all truth."

Extract from a Letter to the Author by the Right Hon. W. E. Gladstone, M.P.:—" I have read every page of the work with great interest, and I subscribe without hesitation to the eulogy passed on it by the *Daily Chronicle*, as making, as far as I know, a distinct and valuable addition to our knowledge of a remarkable period."

"We attach great importance to Mr. Burke's work, as it is, we believe, the first attempt, on any considerable scale, to collect and arrange in a living picture the men and women who made the England of to-day."—*Dublin Review.*

In the Light of the Twentieth Century. By INNOMINATUS. Crown 8vo, 2s. 6d.

"This book is undeniably clever, full of close and subtle reasoning, lighted up with keen epigrammatic wit."—*Literary World.*

NEW MUSICAL WORKS BY

HENRI F. HEMY.

Author of *Hemy's Royal Modern Pianoforte Tutor, &c.*

The Westminster Hymnal for Congregational Use. Part I. Containing 52 Hymns for Advent and Christmas. Price 1s. *Now ready.*

The Children's Musical Longfellow. Containing about 400 Songs. The words from Longfellow. To be published in Shilling parts, each complete in itself, and sold separately. Part I., containing 30 Songs, post free on receipt of 1s.

Carols, Hymns, and Noels for Christmastyde. Selected and Edited by THOMAS WORSLEY STANIFORTH. Price 1s.

"Some of them are very beautiful, and certain to become popular."—*Morning Post.*

JOHN HODGES,

25, HENRIETTA STREET, COVENT GARDEN, LONDON.

www.ingramcontent.com/pod-product-compliance
Lightning Source LLC
Chambersburg PA
CBHW020239170426
43202CB00008B/142